Also by Peter Smith:

Hiring Squirrels
12 Essential Interview Questions to Uncover Great Retail Sales Talent

Peter Smith
Available in paperback and Kindle editions from Amazon.com

"*Hiring Squirrels* is a must-read for any business leader that relies on the effectiveness of his or her sales force. Peter Smith helps to demystify the challenging process of identifying and developing top sales performers."—Bob Blankstein, Management Consultant

"If you want to find real diamonds, read this book. Full of wisdom, practical advice, and engaging stories, *Hiring Squirrels* is told from the perspective of an experienced and exceptionally accomplished professional, and it is sure to help you to identify individuals with true sales talent and bring out the very best in them. Peter Smith's insights can keep you several steps ahead of your competitors."—Patrick Sweeney, Author, *How to Hire and Develop Your Next Top Performer*

"*Hiring Squirrels* should be required reading for any leader of a sales organization that wishes to remain relevant and deliver results."—Hank Siegel, President, Hamilton Jewelers

"There's not much more frustrating and costly than for a manager to hire a new sales associate, spend months and months training him only to find that the person is just not cut out for selling. After reading the book *Hiring Squirrels*, we asked Peter Smith to teach us how to do a better job identifying job applicants. I'm pleased to say that Peter's guidance has saved our company a great deal of wasted time and money."—Jeff Corey, VP Marketing, Days Jewelers

D1314697

"Peter Smith has great savvy and insight into the great game of sales. He is a scholar and a practitioner in the field. This book is filled with his great knowledge and practical know-how. It's a great guide for anyone who wants to be more effective at building a sales team."—Tony Rutigliano, Author, *Strengths Based Selling*

"Wonderful! I think this book should be retitled *The Bible to Seeking, Hiring, Training, and Keeping Productive Salespeople*. Peter Smith is hands down the guru of evaluating sales talent."—Julie Browne, Owner, Sather's Leading Jewelers

"5 stars . . . hands down! There is far more to this book than a list of interview questions. (Though those are worth the price of admission alone)."—Andy Koehn, Owner, Koehn & Koehn Jewelers

"Peter Smith does a masterful job at clearly defining attributes and traits of great sales associates. In this easy-to-read book you will quickly appreciate the simplicity of what really separates champion sales associates from the average, and how to spot them when faced with a hiring decision. Don't wait, take time today to start reading this book. You will not believe its value!"—Dave Padgett, Owner, D&R Diamonds

"*Hiring Squirrels* is the book I wish I had written myself. Concise and insightful, *Hiring Squirrels* should be mandatory reading for all sales managers, HR directors, and anyone else involved in the hiring process."— Jon Walp, General Manager, Long's Jewelers

"Being a professional salesperson in a retail environment is tough; HIRING the right retail sales talent is even tougher. Peter Smith has done the impossible in this book. He has given the hiring manager a list, yes, a LIST of the twelve questions you need in order to identify the right talent. It's incredible to have his insights on this very difficult subject."—Joni Peth, Sales Manager, Kings, Alexandria, VA

"*Hiring Squirrels* offers road-tested lessons to cut through the hype and magical thinking and help you interview, manage, and grow the right talent for your sales team."—Kim Caviness, EVP and Chief Content Officer, Imagination

"Peter thrives at connecting the dots of how to build a team of people that work toward the goal, together, efficiently, and in the roles they are wired to perform."—Ray Lantz, Owner, The Diamond Center

"For most of us in small business, HR is not something we're programed to do well. The book lays out a great set of questions to help in the interview process."—Joel Hassler, Owner, Rasmussen Diamonds

"In a world where goods can be found and delivered from your own home, the real difference maker for brick-and-mortar retailers lies with the consumer experience that the sales associate provides. This is an extremely practical view on how to find and hire the retail sales talent that can make the difference."—Jon Delfino, Vice President Merchandising, Pandora

"It's a great book! *Hiring Squirrels* is a breath of fresh air for anybody in the retail industry—right from the get-go I could not put it down. Overall it is very comprehensive, easy to read, and to the point. A really useful book for anyone in retail management."—Aoife O'Connell, National Sales, Omega, Australia/New Zealand

Sell Something

Sell Something

Principles and Perspectives for Engaged Retail Salespeople

Peter Smith

Copyright © 2016 Peter Smith
All rights reserved.
ISBN-13: 9781537628561
ISBN-10: 1537628569
Library of Congress Control Number: 2016916140
CreateSpace Independent Publishing Platform
North Charleston, South Carolina

"I have to write to be happy whether I get paid for it or not. But it is a hell of a disease to be born with. I like to do it. Which is even worse. That makes it from a disease into a vice. Then I want to do it better than anybody has ever done it which makes it into an obsession."

—Ernest Hemingway

"I have no sense that my feet are touching the ground. I'm elevated to this other space. People say, 'Why don't you give it up?' I can't retire until I croak. I don't think they quite understand what I get out of this. I'm not doing it just for the money or for you. I'm doing it for me."

—Keith Richards

"Every comedian I like does comedy because they *couldn't* do anything else; they were *driven*. They didn't particularly know why, didn't particularly want to do it, but were driven and couldn't *not* do it. Like a calling."

—Billy Connolly

"The idea of sharing singing duties has never appealed to me, in any context. I guess that's why I had never seen the point of singing in choirs. A wonderful Welsh tradition, of course, and I never minded listening to choirs—but how would you get heard in the middle of all that?"

—Tom Jones

Acknowledgements

John Steinbeck wrote, "If there is a magic in story writing, and I am convinced there is, no one has ever been able to reduce it to a recipe that can be passed from one person to another." While humbly ceding to Steinbeck's great and good wisdom, I nonetheless gratefully acknowledge the kind contributions of those who have shared their ingredients with me for this book. If anything was lost, in the recipe or in the baking, the error is mine and mine alone, but the color you have added to my black-and-white ramblings is much appreciated. Thanks to Pat Henneberry, Jim Douglas, Tammy Geraci, Greg McMahon, Brianna Murphy, Lara Lambrecht, Charlene Plaff, Shaina Williams, Bart Marks, Susan Kivlin, Ricky Wubnig, Jodie McRobie, Rich Pesqueira, Michelle Stichter, Eliel Garcia, and Kanye's great friend, Julia Quinn. Also, many thanks to Lindsey Alexander for her great work and to my good friends John McBarron and Jim Lowers, the latter for being a good 'English teacher' when it was most needed. And, last but not least, to my wife and best friend, Sherry, for all you do for me and our little humans.

About the Author

Peter Smith has spent more than thirty years building sales teams at retail and wholesale companies. The Irish native is a graduate of Boston College and is the author of *Hiring Squirrels: 12 Essential Interview Questions to Uncover Great Retail Sales Talent*. Smith is a frequent speaker and panelist, and he is a contributing columnist for *National Jeweler*, *The Jewelry Book* and *World Diamond Magazine*, where he writes about retail, sales-personnel, hiring, and branding.

Contents

In the Beginning

I left school in 1977. I was fifteen years old and I was convinced I was going to play football (or soccer, as it is called in these parts) for a living. School and "real work" just weren't that important in the grand scheme of things. It was the summer of the first *Star Wars* and the first *Rocky* films, and the Sex Pistols, the Stranglers, and Elvis Costello were leading the cultural explosion of punk. It was also the summer that Elvis, *my* Elvis, left the building for the last time, a particularly devastating loss for my fifteen-year-old self.

I did what most fifteen-year-old dropouts did: I bought the *Evening Press* newspaper and turned to the Help Wanted pages hoping to find suitable, or for that matter unsuitable, employment. Anything would do. I don't remember if I was old enough to even shave at that time, but I did have some previous experience, including many house-painting excursions with my dad, and also stints selling soda and snacks door to door. I also had a brief gig working in a van that drove around to different neighborhoods selling vegetables.

I wouldn't say it was *impossible* to find work in those days, but my dad used to joke that it would be better to check the obituary section than the Help Wanted pages. Leafing through the newspaper, I noticed a posting by a wholesale jewelry company that caught my attention for the very best of reasons: there was nothing in it that eliminated me from contention. The company was open to anyone with a pulse, and I had one of those.

I followed directions and took my place in the long line of young hopefuls on Henry Street, on Dublin's north side of town. It wasn't, I discovered, an interview so much as a cattle-call for the masses of young dropouts who assembled outside Connolly's shoe store, above which Novel Jewellery (with its classic British spelling) occupied the second and third floors.

When my turn came, I met the owner, George Pallas, and for reasons not entirely clear to me then or now, he hired me as a stockroom assistant/messenger boy. I was paid the grand sum of fifteen pounds a week, which equated to about thirty US dollars at the time. After giving half of my wages to my mother, I was left with enough to pay my bus fare for the following week and not a whole lot more.

Two things happened the day I got hired at Novel Jewellery. Firstly, I cemented my lifetime love for Dublin's city center or, as we called it, *Town*. And, secondly, I began an unlikely association with the jewelry business that has lasted, as of this writing, almost as long as the aforementioned Elvis lived on this earth . . . *We're caught in a trap, I can't walk out, because I love you too much baby . . .*

I tell that story because it perfectly illustrates how I ended up in this business. I fell right into it. There was no part of me that planned on being in the jewelry business, and there was no inkling whatsoever that I would ever make my living in sales. Like many of you, it happened by chance. If my dreams had been actualized, I'd have been playing midfield for my beloved Liverpool, and for the Republic of Ireland national football team at Dalymount Park and Lansdowne Road in Dublin, and at various stadiums around Europe for millions of adoring fans. But my dreams didn't come true. I didn't get to be a footballer and I didn't get to be a singer, which would have been a fine consolation prize. (*And now, the runner-up prize for career dreams goes to . . .*) I ended up in the jewelry business and ultimately in sales.

You have your own story to tell about how you ended up in sales, and I suspect it didn't feature prominently in your dreams. In the case of my dreams, I continued to play soccer until a couple of years ago, when

I became a danger to myself, yet I am still singing with my trio, although my rock 'n' roll days have long since given way to the softer songs of Frank Sinatra, Nat King Cole, and Tony Bennett. To echo Jack Kerouac, "My fault, my failure, is not in the passions I have, but in my lack of control of them."

I had dinner recently with a retailer friend of mine. "Sales," he said matter-of-factly, "is a place where people end up when they have no place else to go." While I think his sentiment has some merit, I would disagree on a few different levels. In the first instance, it too narrowly defines the role of "sales" as someone who is identified exclusively as a salesperson. I happen to share Daniel Pink's view that we are all in sales. His interesting book, *To Sell Is Human*, talks of a multitude of professions, from attorneys, doctors, teachers, etc., and describes how each of these professions, and many others, requires a level of sales acumen to successfully sell an idea, a plan, or a resolution. To echo Pink, if you are reading this book as a manager, owner, or executive, you too are in sales, regardless of your title.

Many salespeople have done various different things throughout their working lives, only to later embrace a career in sales as a good fit that afforded them a desired quality of life, professionally and personally. That doesn't necessarily mean that they committed to a career in sales because of massive financial rewards, or because it was what they had dreamed about as fifteen-year-olds, but they came to it, at whatever stage in life, because it felt right. These people enjoy what a sales career can provide them and because meeting people, and being on the retail stage every day, aligns with their wiring and personalities.

That said, like me, I imagine many of you fell into a sales career, and it is my sincere hope that reading this book might just be an indicator about how seriously you view your job, your profession, and your commitment to the craft of selling. You will not find these pages to be your run-of-the-mill how-to guide. I don't find those types of books particularly interesting or, for the most part, very helpful. They are usually variations on well-worn themes, and, quite honestly, they often bore the daylights out of me.

What I do enjoy is discussing the things that really matter in sales: understanding whether somebody wants to be in sales or not; whether you can train someone who does not have the right wiring to be a salesperson; how losing feels much worse than winning feels great; how product knowledge can actually be a bad thing, and even how a commitment to serial learning is a must if you are serious about a sales career.

I'm fascinated by the topic of rejection, and how it can drive some to success and yet derail the careers of others, and I'm interested in the Paradox of Choice: how we must have choice, but why too much of it can end up paralyzing us. I am also intrigued about the profound advances taking place in neuroscience, and how findings from the social sciences can help us understand our own behavior and especially that of our customers.

Lastly, I'm passionate about retail and very curious about what it might look like down the road. We are bearing witness to profound changes in retail, and yet there can be little doubt that there will be a place for great retail experiences and great retail salespeople in our ever-evolving future.

In a recently completed study of leading retailers and manufacturers, entitled *Changing the Retail Labor Model for a New Retail Environment*, independent research firm EKN predicted that even with online growth, retail sales in the United States would grow from $3.7 trillion to $7 trillion by 2024, with brick-and-mortar stores accounting for 85 percent of that total. Bain & Company recently predicted that brick-and-mortar luxury retailing would account for 80 percent of all sales by 2025. EKN also noted that the current retail model sees an allocation of only 30 percent of retail labor hours devoted to the top two objectives, sales and customer service. Seventy percent is being spent on operational tasks, with product merchandising being the biggest component—not a good recipe for frontline customer engagement.

Besides the doom and gloom, and the general uncertainty around the massive changes in retail, what seems certain is that brick-and-mortar retail will enjoy very robust growth in the coming years and that salespeople will be some of the most important actors in the evolving model. Doug Stephens wrote in *The Retail Revival*:

There are two things to keep in mind. First, at its core, shopping is a social activity. We shop not only to gather and acquire things we need, but also to commune in public places, to be with people. I'll be the first to argue that online stores will get better and better at fulfilling the distribution aspect of shopping, but I will also hold that nothing will entirely replace the social experience of visiting a market. Second, although the list of things we as consumers are comfortable buying online grows each year, there are still things that are simply more confidently purchased in a physical store setting.

If you are an engaged salesperson, or if you hire and manage salespeople, I hope that you will find this book helpful in understanding what makes great salespeople tick. I specify "engaged" salespeople, as it has been my experience—and the data from numerous studies bear this out—that more than half of all salespeople report they are likely in the wrong job, and, as much as it pains me to say it, I suspect there isn't too much they would get from this or any other book on sales that will fundamentally change that. The assumption is that this book will benefit engaged salespeople who possess the inherent wiring to be successful in sales.

The title itself, *Sell Something*, is intended to cut to the chase of what retail sales ought to be about. When all the dust has settled and the product information and services have been delivered, when the customer has finished their cool bottle of water and the questions have been answered, something needs to have been sold for the business model to work. Be-backs, come-backs, next-weeks just don't get it done. You've got to sell something so the electricity bill gets paid.

If you are, in fact, one of those engaged salespeople, I suspect that some of the material within these pages will inform and illuminate your thinking on elements of sales and consumer behavior, and that it will help you become an even better sales professional. But first, let's take a look at the broader retail landscape.

Retail Salespeople

The Aftermath

As a country, we have emerged from the depths of the deepest recession most of us (hopefully) will ever live through. The recovery, however, will not save the many retail stores who are, without really knowing it, dying a slow death. There are many reasons for the changing retail landscape, and the casualty list is large—and growing. Unfortunately, the default strategy for too many retailers has been simply to stick around until things *return to normal*. Here's a newsflash: things will never return to normal. Normal has given way to a whole new retail landscape that did not start in 2008 with the onset of the Great Recession and, contrary to opinion in some quarters, it did not start in the summer of 1991, when the internet quietly and unceremoniously became available in our homes.

The new normal has been evolving for decades, driven by changing demographics; in particular, the influx of Latino and Asian immigrants; massive changes in media communication and consumption (consider the seemingly infinite number of viewing options on TV alone, where we can DVR shows and avoid watching commercials altogether); and the habits of Millennials, who often watch their favorite shows on YouTube, Hulu, or Netflix, and who get their news on Twitter or other social media platforms, largely bypassing the traditional channels of adverting and messaging.

Other factors contributing to the new normal in retail include the emergence of women in the workplace, as they graduate college in greater numbers than men (even as they continue to strive for equal pay) and shop on a schedule that aligns with their needs, oftentimes far removed from the shopping habits, and hours, of old. For them, it's about shopping on their schedules, not the retailers'.

The decline of the nuclear family has also been a big factor, as we see single-parent families and same-sex families redefine what our new normal looks like. And, of course, the explosion of the aforementioned internet, first onto our desktops, then onto our laptops, and ultimately onto the ubiquitous handheld devices we rely on today. Each has played a part in the ongoing retail revolution.

In recent years in my own industry, jewelry, we have seen huge numbers of previously relevant retailers decide to close their stores, or be forced into closure or even bankruptcy. Some of these retailers made the decision to close their stores because they did not have a succession plan, as fewer and fewer of their children came into the business, and others could not comprehend navigating the changing dynamics of today's retail and decided to call it quits rather than try to reinvent the model.

What used to matter—broad selections of jewelry, gifts, watches, crystal, and even china—just doesn't seem to matter anymore. Millennials can't be counted on to frequent the stores that served their parents. In fact, they can't even be counted on to live in the same geographical area, as many relocate to attend college and don't return to their hometowns at all post-graduation.

As for the younger people who move *into* those markets, well, they have no relationships to or awareness of local retail stores, so they tend to frequent the specialty stores they have become familiar with from their own hometowns. Those specialty stores (whether they sell shoes, clothing, bags, fragrance, makeup, etc.) tend to have a narrower focus, unlike the traditional jewelry store model that communicated, by design or default, that it could be all things to all people.

In their book *Retail Revolution: Will Your Brick-and-Mortar Stores Survive?* Lal, Alvarez, and Greenberg wrote, "Customers are seeking smaller stores that are easier to shop and make better use of their limited time." All things to all people is not a model that works anymore. We've seen it in decline not just in jewelry stores, but in larger department stores that have either been taken over by other companies or gone out of business completely. Stores such as Woolworths, Montgomery Ward, Circuit City, Marshall Fields, Filene's, Bradlees, Ames, and Hecht's all vanished from the retail landscape. And who would want to bet money on Sears or Kmart surviving? Sears might stand as the single best example of a former retail icon that seems completely lost in the changing and challenging retail landscape. As recently as the 1970s, Sears was the single biggest retailer in the world, and one of the top-ten companies on the planet.

There is an argument being propagated by some authors, scholars, and industry consultants that the retail landscape has changed so much that there are only two directions for retailers to go; high or low. On one end of the spectrum, retailers at the mass-marketing level are available everywhere, with a heavy emphasis on discounts and/or low prices and either low service or no service at all; Costco is a good example of this model. On the other end of the spectrum, are premium retailers, which emphasize quality-products that are more exclusive and an outstanding level of service; Tiffany & Co., Nordstrom, Coach and Apple are good examples.

Only time will tell whether the future of retail stores will be defined in such extremes, but I would suggest that if you do own retail stores, you had better pay very close attention to where your store falls on that quality/price continuum. Much of the writing I am seeing on the topic seems to agree that the middle is a veritable dead zone of retail irrelevance. As one retailer said to me recently, "We are all about the lowest price and the best quality." As delusional as this comment is, the scary thing is that his sentiment reflects a default strategy that has many stores believing that they can, in fact, be a great-quality environment while simultaneously competing to offer the lowest price. In Michael Raynor and Mumtaz Ahmed's book, *The Three Rules: How Exceptional Companies Think*, they write:

Our research suggests strongly that the most profitable course of action is to devote your resources to tackling the hard problem of creating anew the non-price value your customers will pay for, not the hard problem of how to remain profitable at lower prices.

Since you are reading this book, I'll assume you are currently working in an environment that is more about the non-price value of retail. For it is in "better quality" retail stores where the need is greatest for a differentiated experience, and these stores are best served by quality, engaged salespeople.

One of the great misconceptions advanced by brick-and-mortar retailers is that they provide great service, whereas their online counterparts do not. Not only is that sentiment self-serving, it is, unfortunately, rarely true. A second myth is that online retail provides no service and, as such, leaves the brick-and-mortar-retailers with a distinct advantage. While some websites may leave much to be desired by way of service, e-commerce giants like Amazon, Zappos, and eBay provide a superb customer experience. In fact, Amazon consistently outperforms brick-and-mortar retailers on the American Customer Satisfaction Index.

Lewis and Dart wrote in their book *The New Rules of Retail*, "Amazon knows all too well that consumers spend three to four times more when having both online and physical stores to shop in." That certainly augurs well for the brick-and-mortar environments, and it underscores the need for great salespeople as absolutely imperative, as this is the single most important differentiator for brick-and-mortar retailers. Of course, to echo Lewis and Dart's comments, any retail store that does not provide an online experience as part of their retail offering is missing the boat.

Inditex (owners of Zara) CEO Pablo Isla has been quoted as saying, "The business is integrated from every point of view," meaning the company does not see e-commerce and brick-and-mortar sales as separate enterprises. Online sales often bring Zara customers into stores, and brick-and-mortar stores often pave the way for online purchasing.

Having two teenagers myself, I can concur completely with Isla's point of view. My kids don't think of online shopping or brick-and-mortar shopping. To them, it's just shopping—and the only factor that matters is what they want and need at the time they decide to shop. Anecdotally, sometimes they ask me to take them to a store and other times they ask for a credit card to buy online. (The credit card requests usually result in a short bout of the cold sweats, and I haven't quite figured that out yet!)

While many factors influence a retailer's growth or, in the worst-case scenario, seal his doom, this book is intended to address one of the most important elements in any retail environment—the sales process, that all-important series of actions that results in someone selling something to someone else in a way that creates real satisfaction for both parties and generates the seeds of future business.

Having great salespeople is fundamental to delivering a great customer experience, and providing a great experience means ensuring that the customer's needs are being met and exceeded. Since few customers visit stores for advice, or to pass time, we must assume that a great experience means they actually bought something. To that end, unless the customer experience consisted of someone pointing to what they wanted and asking for it to be wrapped, it is reasonable to assume that a capable sales professional engaged the customer and successfully managed to exert appropriate influence on his or her buying behavior.

In my book *Hiring Squirrels*, I wrote about the characteristics that are essential to a sales profile. I challenged the way most people identify, interview, and hire salespeople, and, in particular, I called into question the practice of placing too high a premium on experience and too little emphasis on what really matters: drive, empathy and resilience. I argued that those three traits are absolutely critical if a person is to become successful in sales, and I presented the findings of a five-year study I conducted utilizing the Caliper assessments of more than seven hundred retail sales professionals. The salespeople, at the time of assessment, were employed in retail stores across the country. The results of the study revealed that almost six in ten of those salespeople should not have been employed in any sales role whatsoever, let alone one where they were expected to influence a customer's buying decisions. They simply did not have the necessary wiring to be effective in sales, yet many of them were (and continue to be) loyal, educated, and experienced in their industry—all solid qualities suggesting a better fit than is actually the case.

According to the Bureau of Labor Statistics, there are more than 4.6 million people working in retail sales, approximately one-third of whom are part-time. This is a huge number of people, approximately equal to the populations of countries like New Zealand, Croatia, and Ireland. The Hay Group, a management consulting firm, reported in 2013 that retail sales sees a staff turnover of 74 percent. That means that 3.4 million of those salespeople will change jobs in a given year. If I draw from the findings of my work with the seven-hundred-plus salespeople who were tested over five years, and extend that across the broader base of retail salespeople, one might suggest that a full 42 percent of the 4.6 million would have the necessary wiring to be effective in sales, a very robust 1.932 million people. Of course, what that number does not take into consideration is the large number of people who have the inherent wiring to be successful in sales but are working in other occupations. Caliper has typically estimated that number at about 25 percent of the general population.

I should also point out that I am an advocate for part-time salespeople, as I believe that part-timers—far from making up the numbers—actually provide some of the biggest opportunities for retailers if they are recruited, managed, and paid appropriately. Pew Research, for instance, reports that 49 percent of mothers prefer to work part-time. Tapping into that very important base of potential employees is an absolute no-brainer, but it requires a commitment on the part of the employer to craft working hours around the needs of those mothers. Doing so can create a tremendously engaged and—if the hiring process is sound—successful salesperson.

Just a quick note on the whopping turnover of people in sales every year. Much has been written about the enormous costs of turnover. The

Hay Group puts the cost of a single employee leaving at $3,400. While at face value, that's alarming, I think consultants should spend a little more time studying the immense cost of *keeping* the wrong employees. Turnover may not necessarily be a bad thing. If managed properly, it ought to be a strategic part of every business. The operative word, of course, is *managed.* Salespeople who are not suited to the job of selling—a novel concept for the many people employed in sales who believe their primary function is to drown the customer in product information they didn't ask for until they can't take it anymore and, invariably, leave the store empty-handed—cost their companies untold sums in lost business. While it is easy to measure the business that actually happens (sales are down x percent, sales are flat, sales are up x percent), it is mathematically impossible to measure the business that never happened because you had the wrong person in front of the customer.

That lost business happens every single day that your store is open. It happens because customers are not appropriately engaged; customers are not properly listened to; salespeople don't offer open-ended questions; and customers are not asked for the sale. Even when people without the appropriate sales wiring are making sales, they very often resort to the lowest common denominator, the lowest-possible sales return, by delivering lower-average tickets and, in all too many instances, lower-margin products.

So, with the deadly mix of high turnover and the wrong kind of retention, it is clear that there are huge opportunities for motivated retailers to do a better job managing existing team members and to hire better salespeople, both full- and part-time. For salespeople who have the right wiring, there has never been better opportunities to find the best retail environment for your talents, one that gives you the opportunity to make a good living and that celebrates the unique set of talents you bring to the table.

The principle reason for writing this book is to speak to salespeople who do have the necessary wiring and want to be effective in retail sales. Again, this is not intended to be a how-to guide to the chronological steps of a sale. It is a discussion of principles and ideas, peppered with perspectives from retail professionals who were kind enough to share their stories with me.

I will also speak to retail store managers, many of whom come from sales positions themselves, so that they might have a better understanding of how to recognize real salespeople—hey, *someone's* been hiring the six out of ten people who shouldn't be working in sales!—and how to manage them. While the management side of the equation will get less ink in this book, I believe it is useful to speak to those hardy souls. In retail, more than any other sales discipline, the line between what managers do and what salespeople do is often blurred. In fact, there should be a very clear distinction between the two roles; they are as different as any two roles could be.

Amazon That!

If you enter "Sales" into the search field of Amazon's book department, you'll get more than 425,000 hits, and if you have a few moments to spare, spend a little time reading the reviews on some of those titles. As you might expect, you'll see some complimentary comments. You will also find (usually the briefest of reviews) criticism. Those usually go something like this: "It was very basic. Selling 101. I got nothing from it." Or, "If you're just starting out in sales, this is for you." The latter being an example of how "little people" try to make themselves seem important.

For what it's worth, I've observed through the years at seminars, educational forums, and industry events that top salespeople have a natural hunger to learn. They are always looking for an angle, a new way of looking at a problem, a new phrase or piece of language to add to their own toolkit. They are typically not the dismissive one-line-review type of people.

As with most career challenges, there are no silver bullets or magic potions. If the latter group of "superstars" who leave short and dismissive reviews on Amazon were actually deserving of the mantle, they would already know that there are no shortcuts. If they were performing at a very high level in sales, they would be doing so because they executed the fundamentals of sales on a consistent basis and because they challenged themselves every day to make every minute and every opportunity count instead of firing off useless one-line reviews.

Top sales producers know that there are no magic potions to be had, but the best of them are regularly reading books, listening to podcasts and audio books, and watching YouTube videos and TED Talks in an effort to improve themselves. They are always working to enhance their skills, and they absorb their learning in a continuous stream of small, digestible bites. Each positive discovery builds upon previous findings, and it all contributes to a growing professionalism and a level of execution that is consistent and noteworthy.

This book is about introducing and/or reinforcing some basic principles in sales and adding some ideas that have emerged in recent years, thanks to developments in the social sciences. For instance, our ability to utilize fMRI scanning (functional magnetic resonance imaging) to measure how people unconsciously respond to images, words, sounds, and smells has greatly expanded our awareness of how the brain works . . . oftentimes in conflict with our otherwise stated preferences. A neuroimaging procedure, fMRI measures blood-flow to certain areas of the brain and, as those areas light up with activity, reveals a very interesting picture of where and what various triggers are for a given individual, both good and bad, a windfall of useful information in helping us to better understand consumer likes and dislikes.

It's almost as though fMRI has given us a third plane of communication: words, body language, and now neuro-language. Of course, most of us do not have fMRI machines in our places of business, but we can benefit from the mounting data that emerges from that science, data that is readily available to us. We simply did not have the ability to understand these subconscious drivers just a few years ago, but we can now better understand the conscious/unconscious disagreement, as consumers sometimes say one thing while, in fact, believing or doing something else entirely.

I know very smart people who are convinced that retailing today is all about the "deal," in their lingo—they mean the lowest price. They would have us believe that the world has forever changed and nobody, and I mean nobody, pays retail anymore. I often wonder what happens when those people visit places like Apple, Tiffany & Co., and even Starbucks. Heck, even the folks at Dunkin' Donuts will laugh at you if you try to negotiate on your java and bagel.

Weak salespeople, business owners, and managers who claim it's all about price are really saying their store and products either have no value proposition, or, as is more often the case, they do not have the ability to articulate a value proposition with any degree of conviction. One of my favorite quotes of all time came from former US senator John Andrew Holmes, who said, "It is well to remember that the entire universe, with one trifling exception, is composed of others." We would do well to remind ourselves of that sentiment when we find ourselves becoming married to our own narrow biases and prejudices about what customers will or won't buy. It is better to expect the best of them, and to respect them enough to believe that they might be inspired by a competent salesperson who believes in what he or she is selling.

If you sell on price, more power to you. Walmart does a heck of a job positioning themselves as a lowest-cost provider, and if you don't mind walking the equivalent of multiple city blocks to find your "deal" and then waiting an eternity to check out, it might be the place for you. I find that the TJX stores do a very nice job selling off-price. Of course, their model at Marshalls and T.J. Maxx is not for everyone, and there are probably very few things that you would automatically go to those stores for, given the nature of their merchandising strategy. Generally, however, they do an excellent job, and provide a solid value for flexible shoppers.

My wife and I love HomeGoods. You can't really go to HomeGoods and *expect* to find a really interesting end table, but you just might find one if you do. That's their model, and it seems to work pretty well. Going into stores like HomeGoods satisfies two urges: it's got the old-fashioned element of the curiosity store, with the excitement of not really knowing what you are going to find; and if you do discover something you like, you'll probably get a pretty good deal.

For luxury retailing, however, it is not about price, and it frankly can't be about price. You cannot hire talented salespeople, provide an exceptional experience, and sell a great-quality product and make no profit. The math just doesn't work. Raynor and Ahmed wrote in *The Three Rules: How Exceptional Companies Think*:

> There are two dimensions of value along which any company can differentiate itself: price value and non-price value. Our research reveals that exceptional companies typically focus on price value, even if that means they have to charge higher prices. It did not have to turn out this way: price-based competition is a legitimate strategy. We have found, however, that competing with *better* rather than *cheaper* is systematically associated with superior, long-term performance.

I'm a fan of what Warren Buffett's had to say regarding price and value (a distinction that too few people seem to understand): "Price is what you pay. Value is what you get."

A former colleague of mine, Brianna Murphy, shared the following experience that perfectly captures what luxury sales can look like:

> I was recently shopping at Louis Vuitton in Hong Kong. I was not pre-pared to buy anything that day, but the bag I have been craving—and almost stalking online—had been on my mind and I wanted to try it on and have a little test-run with it. I felt like I needed to either grease the tracks of my aspiration—or was it obsession?—or finally pour a bucket of ice water on that particular dream and move on.
>
> In any case, I set off for the huge Louis Vuitton store on Queens Road Central in Hong Kong with my girlfriends in tow. We were greeted at the door by a salesperson who immediately introduced herself and asked what had brought us in. The greet-ing itself was rather routine as welcomes go, neither overly warm nor off-putting. When I described what I was looking for and showed her some pictures on my phone, she led me to a show-case in another section of the shop.

My friends followed, immersed in their respective phones and not really paying much attention to my dreams (since they had not yet dreamed the dream of the Louis Vuitton bag). The saleswoman, Claudia, recognized this disconnect with my friends and proceeded to do something that fundamentally changed the entire dynamic. She first gave each of us a bottle of cold water, worth its weight in gold on a typically hot and muggy Hong Kong day; and secondly, and most impressively, while I was modeling the bag for my friends and for Claudia, she didn't ask me what I thought of the bag—instead she suggested that my two friends take a picture of me with it.

This moment of creativity by Claudia served as a lightning rod to my friends. Suddenly they were excited for me and rattling on and on about how I had to get this bag and how the price really "wasn't that bad." Claudia's tactic worked in two distinct and interesting ways: she managed to get my friends interested in a process that they had been very much on the periphery of, and, whether she knew it or not, she orchestrated a scenario where that picture went viral, almost immediately.

We all use WhatsApp here in Hong Kong so that we can have group-chats and get our community of friends involved in any conversation—and, let me tell you, the bag conversation was a thing. From having no interest, my girlfriends had the photo of me with my dream bag tagged on our WhatsApp group (this particular group includes friends in New York, London, Sydney, Hong Kong, and Singapore). For the next twenty-four hours (while people were waking up in their respective time-zones), I was asked again and again, "Did you buy it?" "You deserve it," "OMG, it looks so good," etc., etc.

Claudia's simple approach was a touch of genius. Instead of flying solo, as the only salesperson involved in the conversation, she got my friends all over the world to influence me by creating a viral permission-to-buy community. To make matters even worse—okay, better, much better—she followed up with me on WhatsApp two days later. I was on a trip and didn't have time to get back to her, but the bag was on my mind.

I did some research too. Should I buy the bag in the US or in Australia during my upcoming trips to save money? I even tried to do that on a trip to Melbourne a short while after. I went into the Louis Vuitton shop on Collins Street, and no one, not one single salesperson, even acknowledged me, which made me think of Claudia back in Hong Kong.

She had earned my business by paying attention to what was going on in my immediate world. She included my friends, who had not been that bothered up to that point, and her attention to detail had resulted in a community of people who were just willing me to buy the bag. In the final analysis, saving a couple of hundred dollars by buying the bag in the US, or in Australia, just didn't seem that interesting to me anymore. Claudia had given life to my little dream, and she would get the sale.

Brianna's story introduces us to a real sales professional in Claudia. She isn't a clerk going through the motions (is there anyone reading this in the Melbourne Louis Vuitton?), she is clearly committed to her profession and serious about what she does for a living. Because she brilliantly read the situation with Brianna and her girlfriends, she was able to sell a bag that could have been bought in another market for less money. I was reminded of Brianna's story recently when reading Martin Lindstrom's new book, *Small Data*. In writing about the habits of Millennials, Lindstrom writes:

> It appeared that every morning, after waking up, the first thing they did was snap photographs of the clothes and shoes they were considering wearing, and text them to all their friends, who would respond positively or negatively. They spent every morning like this, coordinating their fashion choices, using their peers as stand-ins for Anna Wintour, critics who could weigh in not only

about what looked best, but who could also ensure two girls wouldn't show up at school wearing the same shirt, shoes or pair of pants.

Brianna and her friends are a little older than the girls that Lindstrom wrote about, but the principle is very much the same, and the role of social media was never more aptly illustrated.

Many of the sales books I've read suggest that anyone can be trained to be effective in sales, if we just follow whatever recipe the author is selling. I completely disagree with the notion that sales wiring can be trained into an individual who does not have the necessary talent to be effective in sales. To be clear, there are lots of things that can and should be trained: product knowledge, open-ended questioning, overcoming objections, policies and procedures, etc. A full round training on these topics is one way to create the appearance of a solid dance-card, but you won't be dancing very long, or at least not very successfully, without sales wiring. If you are a manager or a salesperson with a desire to learn more about hiring and sales wiring, I unabashedly suggest that you read my book *Hiring Squirrels* for a more comprehensive discussion on this topic.

There are, throughout this book, chapters on elements that have been discussed in other works. Asking for the sale, for instance, is not a new revelation, but it has become more important than ever for two reasons. First, salespeople today are under much greater pressure to close the sale while they have the customer in the store; and second, thanks to the ubiquitous nature of handheld devices, the digital revolution has given customers infinitely more options—information is available immediately. The failure to close now can be fatal in the ever-more competitive world of sales.

Now more than ever, salespeople must be in tune with the customer's needs and much more assertive in closing the sale while the customer is in the store. To do otherwise not only jeopardizes revenue but completely miscalculates the immediacy with which today's consumer expects to be catered to, a theme I explore in the chapter on the customer experience.

Again, consider Brianna's experience in the Louis Vuitton store in Melbourne. Even a modicum of interest on the part of any of those salespeople that day might have resulted in a sale of more than two thousand dollars.

Another theme I explore in the book is client development. Salespeople who do not invest in their customers by seeking to understand and anticipate their needs will quickly lose touch with the realities of today's marketplace. When I go to eBay or Amazon, I immediately see a huge inventory of products that interest me. Their algorithms have built a profile of my preferences, and I am invited to enter a world that seems instantly tailored to my tastes every time I visit these sites. I frequently make purchases that are suggested to me, without having had any intention of doing so prior to visiting these websites.

Another topic that has been written about infrequently, but which ought to be understood in the context of what it may mean to today's customer—and today's salesperson—is the paradox of choice. The paradox is a seemingly contradictory principle by which we want to have choices, we need to have choices, but given too many options, we become incapacitated to the point of purchase paralysis. Another contemporary topic I explore is the contrast principle, the idea that the consumer is better prepared to make a decision not when they're offered the cheapest options, but when they're offered a small number of options that includes more expensive anchor pricing.

Earlier this year, I was giving a presentation in Palm Springs, California, to about a hundred retailers. It was a three-hour presentation, and I was eager to get the audience out of their seats a time or two. I decided that morning that I would try something I had not attempted in any of my previous presentations: I was going to have the audience help me with an on-the-spot research project, and in hindsight, this was a little risky.

I wanted to use the group to establish that our wiring is really a function of genetics, and not nearly as influenced by our environment as we would like to think. To make the point, I asked the audience to stand up if they had two or more children by the same biological parents. About sixty or so people stood up. I then asked if those people would remain standing if they would reasonably describe their respective children as having more or less the same dispositions and personalities.

As the sound of moving chairs filled the room, it became apparent that my worst fears would not be realized. In fact, the result was nothing short of emphatic. Of the sixty or so people who had stood up to indicate they had two or more kids by the same biological parents, all but one sat back down. Every person, with just one exception, had effectively said that their kids had different personalities, different dispositions, despite having been raised in the same household, by the same parents, and with the same value systems.

Every single one of us has unique wiring, and even twins are not an exception to that. The idea that our brain's wiring can be changed or significantly influenced by the home we live in, the parents or siblings who are supposed to help shape us, or the workplace where we spend much of our time is just not supported by evidence from the social sciences. Trillions of dollars are spent each year attempting to effectively change wiring that—as much as this runs counter to the armies of training consultants and companies—is simply not trainable.

I followed up by asking the audience in Palm Springs if they could imagine trying to swap their kids' wiring. Would it be possible, I asked, to make the wiring of one child just like that of their sibling? Without exception, everyone in the audience agreed that the mere idea had no merit whatsoever. The reality, of course, is that our disposition and wiring are very much fixed from shortly after we are born and become more pronounced as we age. Siddhartha Mukherjee wrote in *The Gene: An Intimate History*:

For nearly three decades since the eighties, psychologists and geneticists have tried to catalog and measure subtle differences that might explain the divergent developmental fates of identical twins brought up in the same circumstances. But all attempts at finding concrete, measurable, and systematic differences have invariably fallen short: twins share family, live in the same homes, typically attend the same school, have virtually identical nutrition, often read the same books, are immersed in the same culture, and share similar circles of friends—and yet are unmistakably different.

Understanding that wiring is fixed, even in identical twins, can be a very profound discovery when you are left to lament why one person does well in a sales environment and another does not. It can help to explain why training dollars seem to be well spent on one employee but completely wasted on another. It can help you to understand why the same people seem to win all of the sales contests and why your brilliantly reinvented compensation plan had no effect other than to confirm what you already knew: that the best salespeople continue to be the best, and that those who are not very good continue to struggle, no matter what you do for them.

What we can do, both as potential employers and as employees, is to understand the fundamental elements of our own wiring and to make sure that we find the job best suited to our wiring.

In the next chapter, I will identify the most important traits for the position of sales. If you recognize them in yourself, or in your current or prospective hires, you can rest assured that you have much to work with. If you do not identify with these traits, that may shed some light on why sales has not been the smooth ride you hoped it would be.

This Is Not a Salesperson

Here's a very short primer on what is decidedly NOT a salesperson. If this sounds like you, and you believe you're doing the right things, stop reading this book now and return to whatever it is you were doing before you began reading. I'll break it down into three very simple sentences:

1) **You are not a salesperson if you believe it is your job to save the customer money.**
2) **You are not a salesperson if you think it is your job to tell the customer everything you know.**
3) **You are not a salesperson if you believe the customer always knows what he or she wants.**

I find myself wanting to commit an act of violence (and that's not me, I swear) when I hear so-called "salespeople" tell me they just couldn't bring themselves to charge the customer x or y for a product. Whether that means talking the customer into buying less expensive products or believing it is their job to discount whatever product they are selling, sucking the very lifeblood from a business that is so dependent on ever-declining margins is unacceptable. Those people should be dealt with swiftly and emphatically because they have no business being in sales.

And here's a newsflash: the customer doesn't give a hoot about how much you know. They have better things to do than to listen to your irrelevant diatribe about all manner of stuff they didn't ask about and, more often than not, don't care about. If you are that guy, shut up already!

And finally, if the customer always knows what he or she wants, then why does the business need you? Of course they are not going to tell you they are fumbling around in the dark for that perfect purchase, and of course they are going to pretend they have some idea (nobody wants to look lost), but it is your job to help them get to the place that will make them happy. Even our online purchases are often influenced by the algorithms that shape our experiences. If you are inclined to believe the customer always knows what he or she wants, step away from the vehicle and let a professional take over.

Be Proud or Be Gone

"Our actions are the ground we walk upon."

—Mandy Patinkin

If you are attempting to make a living by selling, then you must completely and without reservation embrace your role as a sales professional. Far too many people believe that being a salesperson is somehow below their dignity, and that lack of pride shows in their performance and in their lack of sales ambition and professionalism.

Great salespeople can earn a good living and can build a good quality of life for themselves. That said, many believe that they have somehow landed on the lowest rung of the retail or business ladder, and they will never maximize their untapped potential if that self-view doesn't change.

One of the ways retail salespeople deal with their own lack of pride is to aspire, whether it fits or not, to a manager or assistant manager position. While that aspiration is in and of itself not necessarily a bad thing, the motives for such an ambition need to be fully understood. If the desire to become a manager is driven by a desire to escape the title of salesperson, then that is a misplaced aspiration.

The very best salespeople should make more money than management, and they should be able to construct a quality of life for themselves without many of the stresses and anxieties typical in managers' jobs.

What's more, a good manager does not require the same skill set as a good salesperson, and it may be a case of "be careful what you wish for" as you find yourself buried in tasks and responsibilities that do not align with your wiring or interests. This is especially true when the manager is expected to personally deliver sales results in addition to leading a team. Add to that, hiring, coaching, firing, scheduling, sales planning, data analysis, customer service, payroll, merchandising, and whatever other responsibilities come with the position, and you begin to understand how completely different it is from a sales role where, by any reasonable definition, the main goals are to move the bar, drive business, and deliver a great experience for the customer.

Of course, it is certainly possible that your wiring is well-suited to management, in which case, chart your course accordingly and refer to the section on management later in this book. If, however, you're more motivated to escape the role of a salesperson, then there is likely a big disconnect that must be reconciled. Either you have the wiring and the desire to be outstanding in sales, or you do not have the wiring and/or the desire, and you should plan on doing something else for a living.

If you want to be a successful salesperson, the first thing you need to do is to make a declarative statement to yourself, and to anyone who might be able to influence and encourage you—your coworkers, manager, family members, etc. Let them know that your goal is to be a great salesperson and that you are prepared to dedicate yourself to accomplishing that end. Philip Delves Broughton wrote in *The Art of the Sale*, "The most significant predictor of performance, the academics found, was role perception. How a salesperson felt about what they did tended to have the largest effect on performance."

Great salespeople are very proud of what they do, and they cherish opportunities to be a part of their customers' lives. They are self-driven, goal oriented, and serious about their profession. They are also dogged in making sure that they are successful, leaving no stone unturned and allowing no opportunity to pass without their best efforts.

If you find yourself shying away from identifying as a salesperson, and frequently thinking about your next position, the next rung of the ladder, or your next job, you just might be in the wrong role, and you may have to ask yourself if you wouldn't be better off in a different line of work.

Profile of a Great Salesperson

"When these results were first published, they astounded even their authors. No one expected such high levels of stability because life experience varies so much. A few people have stable marriages and remain in the same job for a lifetime, but even they see their children grow up and move out, encounter health problems, and live through different political administrations. In 20th century America divorce and remarriage are common, most people change jobs several times, and a typical family moves its residence every few years. People read books, watch television, make new friends. Most people undergo some kind of traumatic experience—an automobile accident, criminal assault, bankruptcy, the death of a relative, a natural disaster, or an act of war. Yet the net result of all these life experiences on personality traits is apparently—nothing."

—DERLEGA, WINSTEAD, JONES, *PERSONALITY, CONTEMPORARY THEORY AND RESEARCH*

DRIVE

There are three defining attributes that all great salespeople share. These attributes are essential; they are not trainable, and they can be present in a salesperson with many years of experience, or in one who has only recently started his or her sales career. A salesperson must have drive, empathy, and resilience.

Drive is the fuel that gets a salesperson up in the morning and keeps that person running all day. It is an inherent characteristic, and it looks different in different people. Some people wear it overtly and seem ever-ready to jump into the fight, leading with a passion and energy that inspires (and sometimes even intimidates) people around them. Others are more subdued in their resolve; they are quietly determined and committed to excellence in sales. One of the great misconceptions about drive is that when it is present, it's present in the most literal sense—visible, audible, and unflagging—and that the person with drive fits a certain model or stereotype, usually that of the attention-seeking extrovert, with limitless reserves of energy.

Great salespeople don't always conform to the extroverted stereotype. In fact, while many extroverts mask as great salespeople—often performing their best work in the interview process—the reality can be very different. Salespeople need to have a combination of extroverted and introverted behaviors so that they can readily switch from the assertive-persuader role to the listening, understanding, and information-gathering role. The best salespeople are really Ambiverts, wholly comfortable in both the performance aspects (communicating, persuading, informing) and the empathic aspects (listening, learning, gathering) of their jobs. We will discuss the idea of Ambiverts a little later.

Drive is not something people choose, like an item from a buffet. It doesn't serve its purposes selectively or sporadically; it is either present in an individual or not. When I speak publicly on this topic, I often ask people to think about their own siblings, or their sons or daughters, to understand the differences in wiring between one person and another.

I was standing next to a parent at my son's high-school soccer match recently, and she openly lamented that she wished her one son had the same "heart" as her other son. She was, of course, talking about their respective exploits on the soccer field, where one son seemed, as she said, to have more "heart" than the other, but I was struck by how ubiquitous drive—or, as my friend called it, "heart"—is in our everyday life. This parent happens to be a soccer coach herself, and she has had plenty of experience coaching kids through the years, including, naturally, her own sons. She wasn't frustrated at the lack of talent, effort, or intelligence from her son that day, she just knew that there was a distinct difference between her two boys, and it seemed to come down to one son just wanting it more than the other. Mukherjee wrote in *The Gene: An Intimate History*:

> Gender. Sexual preference. Temperament. Personality. Impulsivity. Anxiety. Choice. One by one, the most mystical realms of human experience have become progressively encircled by genes. Aspects of behavior relegated largely or even exclusively to cultures, choices, and environments, or to the unique construction of self and identity, have turned out to be surprisingly influenced by genes.

As a soccer player and coach in my own right, I could completely relate to what the mom was saying. I have had the opportunity to play with, and to coach, some outstandingly talented kids through the years, and, long before I ever knew what the missing ingredient was, I often found myself wishing that a certain teammate or kid would just *want it* a little more. This was especially true when the individual in question—as with the son of the parent I was talking to—seemed otherwise to be blessed with great athletic prowess.

Great salespeople are competitive, and many, though not all, tend to have sports backgrounds. They love to compete, they love to win, and they just love being in the game. I love what Babe Ruth said, as quoted in Leigh Montville's great biography *The Big Bam*, "I enjoy being in the game every day, and there is nothing I like better than to get in there and take a hard swing at the ball when some of the boys are on the bases." The Babe, of course, was expressing his desire and passion for competing in game-changing situations.

Naturally, not all salespeople have sports backgrounds, any more than all athletes would make great salespeople. Drive can be found in many other pursuits outside of the sports arena, but a close inspection of a great salesperson's background will likely show clear evidence of a competitive attitude, and that drive has been a major ingredient in shaping who that person is and will become.

Sometimes drive can lead people out of challenging or even tragic life circumstances. It can take kids who, by any reasonable standard, ought to be at a great disadvantage in their family situation (a broken home, mental or physical abuse, or a dangerous community) and give them the needed impetus to rise above their situation and make something of themselves. Drive was likely a big reason that he or she successfully dealt with challenging life situations. It might lead to championing a cause or charity, mentoring disadvantaged children, or volunteering to take on projects that require a great and competitive spirit and a real ambition to succeed. George Anders wrote of Goldman Sachs' recruiting revelation in his book *The Rare Find*:

> Even after Goldman became prestigious enough to hire mostly from the top Ivy League Schools, the firm still prized candidates with scrappy, working-class beginnings. In the firm's formal documents or presentations, this was known as "ambition to achieve." Informally, people spoke of "a lusting enthusiasm to jump out of bed every morning to do the deal."

Drive does not come in a bottle, it cannot be trained, it cannot be bought. (How many creative incentive programs actually deliver lasting change?) It will not come no matter how many great books you read (please keep reading this, though!) or seminars you attend. Drive is fundamental to the role of great salespeople, and it is either present or it is not.

If you do not possess drive, if you are not, by nature, a competitive person (again, this does not have to be in the sports arena), then you will struggle in an environment where you are expected to influence and persuade, to make your sales numbers, and to demonstrate a track record of accomplishment every day.

If, on the other hand, you recognize it in yourself, or, more importantly, if your academic and/or professional journey shows clear evidence of it, you have one of the three most important attributes of great salespeople, whether you currently work in sales or not.

A note of caution: The presence of drive doesn't mean that a given salesperson will always be on their game. The great energy and passion so typical to sales drivers can be tempered if the salesperson finds him or herself in an environment where they do not feel appreciated. Two obvious examples are when they feel like they are working for an ineffective manager, or if they are asked to produce with a compensation system they feel is unfair.

In situations like the above, if they are not corrected in a reasonable period of time, great salespeople can, to paraphrase LeBron James, take their talents to South Beach. Unlike LeBron's example, however, there are rarely such glorious homecomings.

EMPATHY

The second essential element in the trinity of non-negotiables for salespeople is empathy. Nobody without the wiring to listen to the customer is going to have sustained success in sales.

When I was a kid, I would marvel at the showmen who would miraculously appear at local markets. It was as if they had been dispatched from some distant planet that produced all of the carnival and circus people. They would stand in truck beds, hawking whatever wares they had acquired (probably from someone else's truck bed) for that day's work. They were the most fascinating characters, and they had a gift for gathering crowds around them before launching into their confident and lyrical pitch; replete with humor and well-placed flattery, generally aimed at some of the older women present. These characters would sell kitchen tools, radios, watches, pots and pans, towels—just about anything you could think of that could be easily carried away. Standard household items were inexpensive enough to allow for impulse purchases.

The salesmen were always men. They spoke fast. They were funny and always successful in whipping up enough of a frenzy to create an element of urgency with the assembled shoppers, desperate to not lose out on "the deal" from the hawkers. Long before I ever understood that not losing a sale to someone else is a very powerful motivator (more on that later), it was impressive to watch what the silver-tongued and somewhat slippery characters were able to accomplish.

They looked like what I assumed all salespeople looked like, and I could never have imagined being one of them. In fact, I would never have wanted to become one of them. Despite my youth, it was still apparent that there was something just a little bit seedy about them. Their success seemed to hinge upon a strategy designed to get in and get out quick more than anything else. That said, some of their traits are very relevant and very appropriate today. They were great storytellers and showmen, and they had their pitch down so well they almost sang it. Another thing that was very unique about them was that they absolutely expected to make the sale—there were no come-backs, maybes, or next-weeks. In fact, they expected to sell the entire contents of their truck beds, and they were successful more often than not.

What they did not have, however, was empathy. Beyond asking a brief price-related question, customers did not get to talk to them; you simply held your cash out and the exchange was made, quickly and efficiently. The frenzy and sense of urgency created convinced customers that they had to make a decision right there and then. If not, they would lose whatever brilliant cheese-grater was on offer and, worse still, have to watch the person next to them walk away with one instead.

Thankfully, we typically don't have to contend with these characters when we go shopping in better-quality retail stores (although there are one or two retail operations in the jewelry business that come awfully close, with great emphasis on illusion at the forefront of their pitch). Modern salespeople must know how to listen. It is one of the three most important—indeed, non-negotiable—elements in sales, along with drive and resilience, which I'll discuss shortly. If you have great empathy, you stand a very good chance of being successful in sales. Your ability to listen to the customer—and I mean *really listen* to the customer—is central to the skill set of every successful salesperson in every role, retail and otherwise. Satoshi Kanazawa wrote in *Why Beautiful People Have More Daughters*: "A natural empathizer not only notices others' feelings but also continually thinks about what the other person might be feeling, thinking, or intending. Empathy is a defining feature of human relationships and also makes real communications possible."

Empathy means that you listen to what is being said, you intuit what is not being said but could be every bit as important, and you read the customer's body language and tone of voice to really understand how best you can help him or her. Listening means more than staying quiet (and using that time to construct your next statement). It is not a passive act; it requires deep engagement and commitment. It means that you give the customer your full attention and that you, to the best of your ability, block out noise and distractions happening all around you. Leonard Mlodinow wrote in *Subliminal: How Your Unconscious Mind Rules Your Behavior*:

> Scientists attach great importance to the human capacity for spoken language. But we also have a parallel track of non-verbal communication, and those messages may reveal more than our carefully chosen words and sometimes be at odds with them. Since much, if not most, of the non-verbal signaling and reading of signals is automatic and performed outside of our conscious awareness and control, through our non-verbal cues we unwittingly communicate a great deal of information about ourselves and our state of mind.

Listening in sales is not something you can switch on and off. It is not a trait that can be taken out and dusted off for particular customers or on certain days. It is, in the best salespeople in every single industry, an ever-present trait. It is as fundamental to success in sales as anything you could ever do or say, and, most unfortunately, it is not a learned behavior. People without empathy will not be successful in sales. People who are empathic possess one of the three most essential tools to be successful, even if they have never spent a day selling in their lives.

RESILIENCE

The third essential element in great salespeople is resilience. Simply stated, if one does not have the wiring to consistently bounce back from constant rejection and disappointment, he or she will have a very difficult time trying to make a good living in sales.

Even in the most active and robust retail environments, salespeople will statistically have more rejections than sales made. The tally will depend on the particular store. For example, destination stores, where a customer has made the effort to drive to the store, are generally going to have a higher close rate than a store in a mall or a shopping district, where customers may be wandering from store to store, without the same motivation. That said, whether a salesperson is closing 20 percent of customers or 40 percent of customers, he or she had better be able to quickly learn from rejection, forget about it, and move on to the next customer.

Great salespeople derive no more or less pleasure from missed opportunities than do their less accomplished colleagues. The difference between the two groups, however, is that top salespeople do not take rejection personally and they don't allow the misses to influence their attitude or sense of expectation about the next prospect and customer. They file away the miss to be analyzed later, and they move on.

Weak salespeople, on the other hand, have great difficulty with rejection, and they are more likely to take it personally. Consequentially, they avoid getting in front of customers, preferring to let the top salespeople engage them instead, which only exacerbates the performance gap between them. By adopting, usually unconsciously, this attitude of self-preservation, weaker salespeople seek to protect themselves from the ongoing rejections that are inevitable in a selling environment.

A second consequence of this avoidance can be seen when the weaker salespeople do engage customers. While on the surface the interaction may not look a lot different than those of their more successful colleagues, the weaker salesperson will very often avoid asking for the sale. For all the world, they will appear to be friendly and engaging; they will often do a great job providing product information; and their body language and demeanor will suggest a very pleasant experience overall. Not asking for the sale, however, distinguishes the two types of salespeople. One group looks for every opportunity to do it, and the other group avoids it, believing it is the customer's responsibility to tell them if they want to make a purchase.

Managers often see this reluctance to ask for the sale as a training issue, and they invest time and energy working on language, approach, and tactics to improve the close ratio of subpar performers. While those efforts will typically bear fruit with good salespeople, who are eager for any little nugget or tip that will give them an edge, they rarely work with people who do not have good resilience. For them, the issue is not one of training and it is not about motivation. It has more to do with staying healthy, and it goes to the root of their neurological wiring. Bob Rosen wrote in *Grounded*:

> A challenge or threat triggers a survival reflex in the brain, releasing a flood of neurochemicals that throw you into the classic fight-or-flight mode. We all know the effects of chemicals like cortisol and adrenaline. They rev us up, preparing the brain and body for battle or fleeing.

You would, of course, be forgiven for questioning why someone who, it could be said, is actually predisposed to flee from situations where they will be frequently rejected would ever put themselves into a sales environment. (Again, it is their *perception* that they are being rejected personally. Salespeople with great resilience do not see it as a personal rejection.) That is a very reasonable question, and we know that the majority of salespeople should not be working in sales, so lots of people are making strange choices.

In short, without trying to be too simplistic in answering that question, I would suggest that it has much to do with how sales jobs are sold to these people by the managers doing the hiring, and the expectations these salespeople put on themselves when they become salespeople. How often have you asked, or been asked in an interview for a sales position, "How do you feel about customers telling you no over and over again in your work?" Or, "Statistically, you are going to have more failures than successes in this role. Tell me how you feel about that."

I know these questions are a little unorthodox, but they do get to the heart of what resilience is about. Without it, you will simply not be a good salesperson, and you will not enjoy the actual selling aspect of your job. Now, that's where the second component comes in. Most salespeople and, I'm afraid, most managers don't really understand that the single most important aspect of being a salesperson is actually being able to sell stuff. That important detail is often an assumed byproduct of "Do you have experience?" or "How well do you know this product?" That sets up an expectation on the part of the salesperson that being nice, getting along, providing good service, knowing a bunch of stuff, etc., is really what the job is about, and the selling thing . . . well, of course you're going to sell stuff if you are nice and if you love customers. Right? Wrong!

You're going to sell because you are motivated to do so (drive), because you are a great listener (empathy), and because you have the mental wiring to bounce back from the multitude of rejections you receive every day (resilience). These three traits combined will result in your continuing to engage customers and confidently and assertively asking for the sale, without getting bogged down by the inevitable "No, thank you" answers that continue to come your way.

At the Caliper Global Conference in 2012, Herb Greenberg, the late founder of Caliper, said it about as succinctly as one could: "If you are to be successful in sales, you have to be okay with rejection."

AMBIVERTS

I spoke to a retailer in New Jersey recently, and she described an experience she had interviewing a man for a sales position. She described the candidate as a confident, very high-energy extrovert, and she added that he wouldn't have fit in their store as "pushy types" just didn't work for them.

I understood her sentiment, even though I believe it was based on a false assumption. She was correct that a new hire must fit into a company's culture—this is absolutely imperative. The retailer had a very quiet and gentle demeanor, and her disposition seemed to set the tone for her store. The music, the lighting, the colors of the wall coverings, the display elements, and, on first glance, even the other employees all communicated a quiet calmness. The candidate she described might have turned out to be a bull in a china shop, and, no matter how accomplished he might otherwise have been as a salesperson, he was probably not going to be a good fit.

On another level, though, one could debate whether the subdued environment in the store was conducive to maximizing sales opportunities, as it certainly didn't strike me as appealing to younger buyers. But I digress. The false assumption I referenced was the retailer's belief that the candidate would be good in sales just because she identified him as an extrovert. Most of us tend to infer that good salespeople are necessarily extroverted. How often have we heard the expression, "He could sell ice to the Eskimos?" That expression is usually pinned on people who are outgoing, talkative, and generally comfortable in social situations.

The problem is, however, the assumption is just not accurate. Believing that all good salespeople are extroverts, or that all extroverts can be good salespeople, satisfies a very surface-level instinct about salespeople but it is not always the case. The candidate the retailer mentioned was driven; he projected a confident persona and seemed to be a good communicator. Those would appear to be good qualities for a salesperson, but there are two crucial elements the retailer had not investigated or understood. One was whether he had resilience. How would he react to the rejection that is so inevitable in sales? All the bravado in the world will not compensate for wiring that does not handle rejection well.

The second element her interview had not uncovered was whether the candidate was a good listener or not. If he did not possess empathy, the ability to listen, to read body language, to intuitively infer the needs of customers, he would not be a successful salesperson. All the bravado and extroversion in the world really only serves to mask those fatal shortcomings.

Adam Grant from the Wharton School wrote a seminal white paper ("Rethinking the Extraverted Sales Ideal: The Ambivert Advantage") that spoke to the power of neither extroverts nor introverts but what he called Ambiverts. Grant wrote:

> Ambiverts achieve greater sales productivity than extraverts or introverts do. Because they naturally engage in a flexible pattern of talking and listening, Ambiverts are likely to express sufficient assertiveness and enthusiasm to persuade and close a sale but are more inclined to listen to customers' interests and less vulnerable to appearing too excited or overconfident.

We are culturally more familiar with the introvert and extrovert labels, therefore, it is understandable that we would be more apt to believe the latter have the necessary qualities for sales, while steering clear of the former, believing they just don't have the get-up-and-go to be successful. Despite the stereotypes, when you consider what great salespeople actually look like, they don't necessarily look like the interview candidate, bold and brash. They are, as Grant concludes, adept at both talking and listening, with the ability to drive the conversation to a successful conclusion far more often than their more extroverted colleagues. Daniel Pink wrote in *To Sell Is Human*: "One of the most comprehensive investigations—a set of three meta-analyses of thirty-five separate studies involving 3,806 salespeople—found the correlation between extraversion and sales was essentially nonexistent."

Grant's own study of more than three hundred salespeople over a three-month period showed that Ambiverts outperformed introverts by a whopping 24 percent, and—wait for it—they outperformed extroverts by 32 percent. So, the next time you want to ascribe great sales attributes to an outgoing personality, stop for just a minute and ask yourself if there is clear evidence of them also being a good listener. The good news is that personality psychologist Robert McCrae told the Huffington Post that he estimates 38 percent of us are Ambiverts. Now, if we can just figure out who is in the 38 percent group so we can avoid the 62 percent, like that guy in New Jersey.

BAGGAGE

With the exception of Southwest Airlines (as of writing), checking your baggage costs money. I still remember the day I realizes baggage charges were coming as though it was yesterday. I was checking myself onto a Delta flight—remember when people used to do that for us?—and I noticed a new icon on the Delta check-in screen. In the section where I indicated I was checking a bag, it said "Free." My heart sank. There is no free lunch, and I knew at that moment that the days of paying to check luggage were fast approaching.

Great salespeople come with baggage too and it is never free. You have to pay a price one way or another, and, in the vast majority of cases, it is worth every penny of that cost. Sometimes that baggage looks like t's not being crossed and i's not being dotted. Sometimes it can look as though your top salespeople are self-servingly profiling, as they quickly scan and dismiss prospects they deem not worthy of their attention.

At other times, that baggage comes in the form of intolerance, either of a poor manager or of their less-accomplished colleagues. It is worth noting here that nearly all the research tells us that salespeople don't leave companies, they leave bad managers, so if that relationship is strained, it can result in an unwanted vacuum. The salespeople who are easier to manage because they have less baggage are not usually great sales producers, and they do, unfortunately, tend to stick around for years. Not,

I would suggest, the kind of employee retention that is always good for your business.

Rather than attempt to mold the perfect employee, great managers know to check their egos at the door and learn to manage the baggage. They do it by keeping the challenges of managing top performers in perspective; by recognizing that the upside of outstanding performers far outweighs the downside of a little baggage; and they do it by creating the kind of workplace that plays to the strengths of the most effective salespeople, despite having to mitigate their baggage.

Great performers tend to be passionate people; they love what they do. They see what they do as a calling more than a job, and their emotional character can be both positive and negative. They are serious and committed to their tasks, and they typically demonstrate a low tolerance for things that get in their way. This very often entails a certain level of frustration for non-sales-related tasks. Taking top salespeople off the sales floor is like taking fish out of water. They will struggle to get back where they belong, in the middle of the action, where they can make sales happen.

The best environment for a top sales producer is one where they can do their best work. They do not want to be managed the same way as people who are not top performers, and the more you attempt to mold them into an image of what you think a great salesperson ought to be, the quicker you will sow the seeds of unrest and discontent.

When I think back on all of the environments, retail and otherwise, I have worked in, there were always one or two real sales drivers. They were rarely the most popular members of the team (at least with their coworkers), and they were never the easiest people to manage. They were, however, always the very people we turned to when business needed a turbo-charge. Steve Suggs writes in *Can They Sell*:

> Many times, sales managers tell me they want salespeople who are coachable, and who are team players. In response to this common statement from sales managers, I say, "No, you really don't."

When I explain the advantages of recruiting salespeople who are prone to be independent and hard to coach, they agree with me. You really want someone who is a challenge to coach but who listens.

Someone who manages salespeople must also establish an environment that supports the best producers, one that is free of snide criticisms from coworkers who see decidedly less value in the determined and focused way in which top performers operate. As obvious as that may seem, I have witnessed entirely too many workplaces over the course of my career where criticizing the best people seems to be its own sport. That particular Greek chorus is usually made up the non-performers, and it generally centers on the star performer's shortcomings in non-sales areas: fixing displays after they have worked in a given area; doing their share of housekeeping, etc. Another popular sport is complaining about the direct manner in which top performers pursue customers and their obsession around meeting and exceeding sales goals. As a manager, it is essential that you stamp out negative rhetoric before it becomes a cancer that results in a far bigger and more costly separation, as top performers seek an environment that is more supportive of and friendly to their unique talents.

Body Language and Appearance

"If you are smiling together, you are usually in harmony."

—ANN DEMARAIS, VALERIE WHITE, *FIRST IMPRESSIONS*

We all make choices about what to wear every single day. For some, it starts with what is passable, pressed, or clean, and for others it is more of a ritual, with careful thought and attention given to the coordination of that day's outfit. I've got my own idiosyncrasies: I like my belt and shoes to match, I cannot stand to have scuffed or unpolished shoes, and I always wear French-cuff shirts when working. Beyond that, I'm generally not the kind of dresser that will stand out for good or bad reasons.

I have a former colleague, Susy, who is extremely stylish. In fact, I'm not sure that I have ever seen her wearing the same outfit twice, and she always looks good. I've known her for about ten years, which must mean, I've concluded, that she has to have at least two thousand different outfits and an awfully big closet—more of a walk-in closet-house.

Whether you are in my camp or Susy's, it should be a given that when we do arrive at work and prepare ourselves for that day's appearance on the great retail stage, we should look like we are there to work. Taking the time to pull yourself together shows respect for your colleagues and your customers. Dressing and looking the part has also been proven to significantly increase the likelihood of you being viewed more positively by your customers, your colleagues, and your employers. It's called the "halo effect," and it has been scientifically proven that people who look like they have it together are generally thought of as, well, having it together, even if that isn't always the case.

I know there is a tendency by some to view dressing for the part and looking great as being consistent with good looks, the ideal body shape, and other attributes sometimes more closely associated with the gene-pool lottery than with personal choices. Nothing could be further from the truth. Every single one of us can make a huge difference in how we are viewed by exercising good judgment in the choices we make about our personal wardrobe and our grooming habits. Paying attention to a few little details can make a very big difference in how we are perceived.

Once you have dressed for the part, the next thing to do is to act like you want to be there. I am a committed and passionate admirer of great retail experiences, and I love when I see and sense great energy from retail sales professionals. In fact, I would argue that a great retail salesperson can mask a great many sins if he or she has the right attitude. Their body language can transmit such warmth and sincerity that, as a customer, you can unconsciously find yourself under their spell, and, as such, you are much more inclined to make a purchase and return to that store and to that salesperson, again and again.

There have been numerous studies in recent years that focus on mirror neurons, how we unconsciously mirror the behaviors and actions of others when we engage with them. If they are happy, we are more likely to be happy; if they are sad, we too tend to wear a sad face. If they are angry, well, that just makes us angry, too. Susan Cain wrote in *Quiet*, "Studies show that taking simple physical steps—like smiling—makes us feel stronger and happier, while frowning makes us feel worse."

Have you ever found yourself listening to someone talking with a stutter? What do you find yourself doing? We know, of course, that it is neither politically correct nor helpful to stutter along with them, or to finish their sentences for them—and yet many of us have to suppress the urge to do so. Have you ever tried to prevent yourself from yawning when someone you are with is yawning?

"Mirroring" speaks to our desire to be *empathic* and to align in a social context. Mirror neurons are at work every time we engage another human being, and our desire to be accepted and liked is deeply rooted in our subconscious, a product of evolution itself and as important as our need for food and shelter. Since the beginning of time, being accepted by the tribe or community was often the difference between life and death. Someone who wasn't accepted into the tribe was not afforded the safety that came with numbers at a time when we were either the hunter or the hunted. Ann Demarais wrote in her book *First Impressions*, "You may assume that someone who appears upbeat is also smart, likeable, and successful, even though you've never seen evidence of those qualities in her."

People also tend to see negative traits in the same manner. The opposite is the halo effect is the "horns effect." Demarais' horns effect perfectly describes those retail salespeople who choose, for reasons that will always confound me, to bring a negative attitude and demeanor into their place of work. As certain as I am about positive transference, the same applies to negative transference, and, of course, the difference between them really boils down to mindset. You are going to reflect the attitude you choose to bring to work, and that, consciously or otherwise, is what gets communicated to your customers and colleagues.

One of the easiest and most effective tools to engage people around you is, quite simply, smiling. Wearing a smile accomplishes two very important ends. In the first instance, it transmits, through the power of the aforementioned mirror neurons, a very warm and welcoming attitude to the person you are talking to. It is difficult to be miserable when you are talking to someone who is happy (the opposite of "misery loves company"). You will find yourself slowly but surely succumbing to the attitude of the other person if they are in an authentically good mood. I say authentically as there are stores that do a better job of training their salespeople than they do hiring the right people in the first place. That combination of good training and bad recruiting can fill a store with people who don't want to be there and who go through the motions as if they are checking a box on a questionnaire. As Rosabeth Moss Kanter wrote in *Confidence*:

> "Primitive emotional contagion" is the unconscious tendency to mimic another person's facial expression, tone of voice, posture, and movements, even when one is focused on other things and is seemingly unaware of the model for the mood. The synchronizing of a sad or happy tone of voice, for example, is often unconscious, as though the human brain is hard-wired to get in tune with other people, because it is more pleasant to have a sense of rapport. Being out of tune is jarring and makes people feel isolated.

Wearing a smile and carrying an upbeat, positive attitude works more often than not in transferring your mood to your customers. An exception to that is when a person you are trying to engage with brings a dominantly negative attitude into the interaction. In such cases, you can and should attempt to diffuse the situation with positive words and body language. However, despite our best intentions in situations like that, the most dominant personality will usually prevail. That means if your positive and upbeat demeanor is consistent and real, you will begin to win the customer over. If, on the other hand, his or her negative demeanor is more powerful, you will have an interesting but not necessarily insurmountable challenge on your hands.

The second very powerful aspect of wearing a smile on your face is that it has been clinically proven to lift your spirits. It has long been thought that our faces express our feelings. More recent works in neuroscience, however, posit that the opposite is also true, that our faces, in fact, can lead to and ultimately determine our mood. Think about how powerful that finding is, that we can decide we will be in a good mood and that we can get there by smiling. David Lewis wrote in his wonderful book *Impulse: Why We Do What We Do without Knowing Why We Do It*, "When we see someone smile, our mirror neurons for smiling also fire, creating in our mind the emotions associated with the smile. There is no need for us to think about the other person's intentions behind the smile—the experience is immediate and effortless." With so much at stake, can we afford not to smile?

Jodie McRobie is one of the most upbeat salespeople I have ever met. I was buzzed into her store in Ohio one afternoon, after a truly miserable experience in another jewelry store earlier that day, and I found myself immediately drawn into her web of energy and positivity. She approached my colleague and me as if we were long-lost friends, all the while exuding an authenticity and optimism that was impossible not to like.

We've all been in situations where we are approached by an energized, almost manic, salesperson, whose best efforts to sound authentic fall flat. It's as if they are trying to become your best friend before you even say hello, and it comes across as shallow and misguided. Well, that's not Jodie. Her energy and genuine love of meeting people and engaging with them is nothing short of infectious, and she very quickly brightened my day with her good humor and great attitude.

After we had visited for a while, I made a point to compliment Jodie on how she had greeted us when we entered the store. She had no idea who we were, and yet we were greeted in such a warm manner that we immediately felt welcome. She thanked me for the compliment and said she loved what she did and that she tried to greet everyone that way. She told me the following story to illustrate her point, and I should point out that her store is in a downtown that has its challenges and, as such, customers need to be buzzed into the store.

It was typical day here when our doorbell rang. I buzzed the guest in and greeted an older African American man. He was new to our store, and he asked if he could look around because he wanted to buy himself a nice watch and chain. Of course I invited him to do just that, and we began a nice conversation as he did so. He seemed a little unsure of himself in the store, and his attire had clearly seen better days. It was clear to me, however, that he really seemed to appreciate the welcome and my efforts to engage him. As we spoke, and I got to know him a little more, he volunteered that he had, just the previous week, won $250,000 on a lottery scratch ticket. I had never met anyone who had won that kind of money before, and I let out an unbridled "YESSSSSS" . . . which made him laugh, embarrassed me, and brought the owner of the store running from the back room.

As the conversation continued, I learned that the man had once been homeless and that he was now starting to turn things around; even attending classes at a local college. He talked about his plans to buy a durable used car, two nice suits, and the two aforementioned indulgences—a watch and a chain.

As we were talking, an officer walked into the store, and she was talking about a homeless donation drive she was in charge of. My customer reached into his pocket and made a donation right there and then.

As exciting as it was for my customer to have won the money, he gave me a wonderful gift that day. I was reminded about the value of treating everyone with the same respect and dignity that I want for myself, and of approaching every customer with a desire to learn a little something about them, and to give each one of our guests a nice experience in our store. He did make an important purchase that day, perhaps the biggest of his life, but he left something much more important for me, and for that, I will be forever grateful.

There is so much to love about Jodie's story. Having experienced her warm greeting and her great body language firsthand, I could only imagine how refreshing that must have been for a man not used to visiting jewelry stores, let alone those where he had to be buzzed in. I loved how she tried to get to know the man, when so many might have eyed him suspiciously, not ever imagining that he could have afforded to make a purchase. I loved how she listened to him so that she was able to discover that he was, even in his advanced years and in challenging circumstances, attending college classes. And most of all, I loved that Jodie got such a great reward for the great energy and attitude she so routinely brings into every customer interaction.

Connie Dieken wrote in *Talk Less, Say More*, "People give back to you what you give to them. Energy feeds on itself. Energized people create energy in others." Jodie's story is a great example of this. Being positive and communicating, both verbally and with your body language, is all about choice. It may not deliver you a lottery win, but the rewards to your business for making the right choices are plentiful.

Serial Learning

"Some people die at twenty-five and aren't buried until seventy-five."

—BENJAMIN FRANKLIN

I walked onto the campus at Boston College in Chestnut Hill to take my first-ever college class at thirty-two years old. I was a lifetime removed from that June day in 1977 when I left Ballymun Comprehensive School in Dublin for the last time. It was the first step toward my undergraduate degree, a journey that would take up every spare moment of the following six years. I was as nervous as anyone could be, and I wondered if I could hack it, or if I would embarrass myself in front of a room full of strangers. The classroom was located in Fulton Hall, one of BC's magnificent Gothic Revival buildings, and the structure both inspired and scared the living daylights out of me. *This is what college ought to be like*, I thought, but me being in such a fine institution of learning wasn't something I had ever allowed myself to even dream about. Professor Jim Murphy walked in, looked around the room, and offered a warm good morning, followed by his best "Judy, Judy, Judy" impersonation of Cary Grant. Life had never been better.

As I mentioned at the beginning of this book, I took a job with Novel Jewellery while I waited for the call to go to England to play soccer. I did whatever needed to be done, including making the tea, running packages to the post office, and making endless trips to the Assay Office, those stellar guardians of metal integrity, and the bane of our existence. (Have you ever had to untangle gold chains for eight straight hours?) While I perfected my tea-making, package-wrapping, and bringing-stuff-to-the-post-office skills, I fell in love with my hometown of Dublin, as I traversed north and south of the River Liffey on all manner of errands, or "messages" as we called them then. All the while, I continued to dream my dream of playing football for a living.

Thankfully, I also had the uncommon good sense to make a habit of reading books at every opportunity, and I embraced that commitment with a passion. Professor Arthur Cullman of The Ohio State University once said, "Change is a habit, and you have to get in the habit of it." Without question, I got in the habit of reading, and this lifelong passion has, I am delighted to say, survived the digital age. There are no plaques at Ballymun Comprehensive to mark my contributions. My commitment while attending school was to maximize every available minute to play soccer, and to minimize every obligation to do any schoolwork. It was, in many respects, a perfect storm. I didn't want to be there, and they didn't care if I was there or not. I was just another Ballymun kid being spit out into the real world to deal with whatever life threw at him.

In any case, whether it was a happy accident or a moment of divine inspiration I will never know, but determining to read as much as I did at that early age set me on a course of lifelong learning that feels as fresh and relevant today as at any time in my life. My ongoing journey of learning echoes Albert Einstein, who said, "Education is what remains when one has forgotten what one has learned in school." I had, to be fair to Albert, very little to forget.

Whether you have multiple college degrees or you are a high-school dropout, if you are serious about becoming a great sales professional, you must commit to continually learning, expanding your knowledge and understanding of sales and consumer behavior. Things are changing at a rapid pace, and you must continue to push yourself to learn more, to better yourself, to make the experiences ever more positive for your customers. You don't have to be a voracious reader of books, but you must utilize the many different sources of learning that can, thankfully, be digested in small bites to suit your own schedule and learning style.

Social media such as Twitter, Facebook, and LinkedIn provide an endless pipeline of interesting content from all manner of sources. In a very short period of time, you can Like and Follow sales trainers and influencers, business and neuroscience magazines, universities and news outlets—and you can stay current on ideas, discussions, and developments in sales and related areas of interest in just a few minutes a day.

Salespeople who are not driving themselves to become better at their profession will never perform at the top of their game. Quite frankly, there is no excuse whatsoever for not staying current, given the vast majority of sources available today, whether you learn through books, online sources, podcasts, or continuing education. There have been so many advances in the study of consumer behavior in recent years, and the only thing we can be certain of anymore is that change is a constant.

Not long ago, shopping was a much more relaxed pastime. Customers seemed content to amble from store to store, and they were often happy to almost hang out in stores for extended periods of time. Shopping today seems more like an Olympic event, with customers flying in and out at warp speed, all the while checking their handheld devices to ensure that they have the most up-to-date information and the best prices. Changing consumer behavior cannot be understood by applying dated practices and attitudes; you simply must stay current.

The next time you attend a conference or any kind of educational event, check the front row. Look very carefully at the attendant faces in the seats closest to the speaker. They are the best salespeople. The very people that you would think would need ongoing education the least are often the good souls filling the front rows. That is no accident. They are top producers because they see themselves as professionals and because they choose to embrace every opportunity to give themselves even the slightest edge.

If you have not yet committed to a habit of learning, then change that today. Make a decision to read something or learn something every single day. Whether that is reading more books on selling or consumer behavior; industry journals; related magazines; or the multitude of online resources, there is, quite frankly, no excuse for not committing yourself to a path of growth and development.

If you put the word *sales* into a TED Talks search, as of this writing you will uncover 159 results. The word *customer* in the same search gives you 119 results. If you want to delve a little more deeply into consumer behavior, put *neuroscience* into the search and you will get another 244 results. My point is, if you did nothing more than watch one TED Talk per day on a related topic, you would expand your knowledge base immensely and, I suspect, increase your interest in furthering your learning, as you will have exposure to great writers, influencers, thought leaders, and educators.

I'll leave the final word on this topic to Bob Rosen. He wrote in his book *Grounded: How Leaders Stay Rooted in an Uncertain World*, "If you are continually curious, this strengthens your brain's wiring and communication systems. The opposite is true, too. If you do not stretch your brain, certain regions atrophy. This is the principle behind the 'use it or lose it' mantra."

The principle behind serial learning is not that you accumulate an arsenal of facts to use as weapons, but that you develop a habit of curiosity about sales, sales processes, body language, consumer behavior, and specific industry-related topics and learning that will contribute continually to your personal growth and development, whether you are new to sales or have twenty or more years of experience. If you are fortunate enough to work for a company that provides those opportunities, embrace them completely.

Optimism

"We live in the world when we love it."

—RABINDRANATH TAGORE

Where do you think the expression "misery loves company" comes from? Why does it seem to be so true, and why don't the people who are in that club ever recognize themselves for what they are? Miserable. For the record, I will state without reservation that I am pathologically predisposed to avoiding negative people. I'm fairly certain that my condition is deeply rooted in my genes, and I don't want a cure for it. I want to stay this way. I never want to be okay being around negative people.

There has to be a perfectly logical explanation as to why negative people find comfort in the company of other negative people. Perhaps it has something to do with them being able to *fail* quietly, away from the winning glow that their more successful and more engaged colleagues cast. Maybe it's an unconscious choice to become comfortable in failure, rather than put too much pressure on themselves to be successful. If that's the case, one could understand why someone with a similar negative demeanor would find comfort in that club. It's a little bit like running a race and, no matter how far back in the field you are, you console yourself by checking the number of runners behind you, instead of reaching for those ahead. Rosabeth Moss Kanter wrote in *Confidence*:

Psychologists use the term "defensive pessimism" to describe the way some people set low expectations to cope with anxiety in risky situations. This set of people is not trying to make excuses or deny responsibility; they just prefer to expect failure, so as not to be totally debilitated by anxiety about whether they can meet a lofty goal.

Whatever the reason for a negative mindset, there can be little doubt that it is never a good strategy for sales success. No one will ever be inspired by your dour demeanor, your excuse-making, or your glass-half-empty attitude. I once remarked to someone I worked with that one of our colleagues, someone in a position of significant influence, seemed to view every glass as half-empty. The person I was talking to shot back, "You are wrong. He sees every glass as two-thirds empty." The sad truth was, this guy was the boss of the negative ninny, and yet he seemed content to have someone who frequently demotivated his people in a senior position. Culture be damned, I tell you!

Here's the good news: Being negative is a state of mind. One can arrive at negativity via many roads, but it is always within your power to get yourself into a more positive mindset and to live your life accordingly. A big part of that means that you have to decide to seek the positive in situations and people, and find a way to rid yourself of negative people. Life is too short to be pulled into the mire by people who think it's their role in life to point out everything that can and will go wrong.

We have all heard the phrase "You don't choose your family, but you do choose your friends." Nothing could be more accurate than that statement. It stands to reason that if you surround yourself with positive, optimistic people, their excitement, their energy, and their ambition will rub off on you, you will expect more of yourself, and you will more often find yourself in a better place and mindset. You might even find yourself having a laugh at yourself every now and again instead of becoming vexed or upset about something.

If you are a negative person, change your mindset now, and, if necessary, change your circumstances and even your friends. Nobody should ever feel obligated to maintain relationships that are inherently draining. While your loyalty to negative people may gain you sainthood, it will not improve your quality of life, and it will not serve as fuel for positive experiences for you, your colleagues, or your customers. If your negative friends are sincerely interested in maintaining a relationship with you, tell them that you need them to be more positive and that you won't allow yourself to be dragged down. If they are not responsive to that message, you have every right to change that relationship.

I worked for a company many years ago that was perhaps not the most pleasant place to work. I was surrounded by great people, but far too many of them allowed themselves to be pulled into a negative web. I resolved that I wasn't going to fret the things that I had no control over, I was going to focus on being positive, finding the good (and there's always lots of good to be found) in my day and in my job, and not allowing myself to descend into whatever pity party was happening on any given day.

I remember having a conversation with some of my colleagues and resolving that we needed to work on the things that we could control and not become obsessed by the things we had no control over. A group of us agreed that we would try to have lunch together once a week and that, as a rule, you could not bitch, moan, or complain about company business at that lunch. We were going to enjoy the heck out of each other's company and laugh as much as we could. It worked. Those lunches were a great deal of fun, and we were able to put our frustrations aside for an hour or so each week and just enjoy that welcome respite.

If your situation at work is bad, take the necessary actions to change it. Go to your manager and propose some actionable steps that might help to create a more pleasant working environment. If your suggestions are reasonable, and you get no joy from your conversation with your manager, you might want to begin looking for a new job.

If, on the other hand, you have become a part of the problem, you have made the decision to be unhappy, to refuse to lead positive change, then you must accept responsibility for your action or inaction. Honestly look in the mirror and ask yourself if you could be handling situations better. Could you make more of an effort to connect with the more optimistic and successful people in your company, or have you defaulted to the misery club?

There is no excuse for and no joy in living with a negative mindset. A miserable place to work saps your energy and that of your colleagues and customers. We're all smart enough to think of a dozen reasons to justify why we might be negative, and why we don't like what we are doing and/or who we are doing it for, but all it takes is one reason to become more positive, one reason to shed the cloak of negativity and disengage from the people who have jumped on that negativity bandwagon. Your mental and physical health will thank you for choosing to lead your life as an optimist, expecting the best of people and situations and occasionally making lemonade when you're handed a bag full of lemons. Bob Rosen wrote in his book *Grounded: How Leaders Stay Grounded in an Uncertain World*:

> Positive emotions also help protect you against heart disease. A ten-year study in Nova Scotia found that people who are happy, enthusiastic, and content are less likely to develop heart disease. Furthermore, people who are in a good mood every day and use humor to cope have a stronger immune system.

A guy I used to work with had the habit of saying, "You'll always know where you stand with me because I'll always tell you what I'm thinking." On the surface, his reminders (to paraphrase Billy Crystal's character in *The Princess Bride*) were intended to be a "mostly" good and "mostly" reasonable testament to his candor. Alas, for me, what I was hearing was "I am not a positive guy, and I will tell you now—and again and again—that I'm going to be complaining a lot. In fact, I'm a negative so-and-so, and I'm hoping that my frequently couching it as candor will give me a license to be negative all the time." As a wise man once said, "Yeah, no thanks. I'm not having it."

My thought was that he was just making excuses for his failures. He was lining his pockets with justifications and rationalizations before even getting into the game. I told him as much, and I reminded him that he needed to get himself to a place where he expected success, or we wouldn't be working together much longer.

I am 100 percent convinced that we have more success by expecting it than by expecting to fail. I don't know how much more success, and it certainly varies from person to person, but those salespeople who expect great things of themselves will always outperform those who do not. Brian Tracy wrote in *Be a Sales Superstar*:

Top salespeople believe in their companies. They believe in their products and services, and they believe in their customers. Above all, they believe in themselves and their ability to succeed. Your level of belief in the value of a product or service is directly related to your ability to convince other people that it is good for them.

It may be true that some people are born optimists and some are born pessimists. My own mother used to say, "He's not happy unless he's moaning." That's an Irish way of saying that someone is generally not content unless he or she is actually being miserable. Again, whether one is born with a slant toward negativity, positivity, optimism, or pessimism is above my pay grade. What I do know is that we choose the company we keep, we choose the material that we do or don't read, and we choose whether to allow pitfalls and setbacks to define us or drive us forward. Daniel Goleman wrote in *Emotional Intelligence*:

Just why optimism makes such a difference in sales success speaks to the sense in which it is an emotionally intelligent attitude. Each no a salesperson gets is a small defeat. The emotional reaction to the defeat is crucial to the ability to marshal enough motivation to continue. As the no's mount up, morale can deteriorate, making it harder and harder to pick up the phone for the next call. Such rejection is especially hard to take for a pessimist who interprets it as meaning, '"I'm a failure at this; I'll never make a sale."'—an interpretation that is sure to trigger apathy and defeatism, if not depression. Optimists, on the other hand, tell themselves, '"I'm using the wrong approach,"' or '"That last person was in a bad mood."' By seeing not themselves but something in the situation as the reason for their failure, they can change their approach in the next call. While the pessimist's mental state leads to despair, the optimist's spawns hope.

There are some people I would call exhaustive optimists. What I mean by that is they are so overtly driven to see everything in a positive light that it quite simply wears me out. These are not the kind of people that I am referring to when I advocate for optimists in sales. There needs to be some balance, some acceptance that bad stuff will occasionally happen, and we should be honest about that. The dogged optimists seem to embrace an overly dramatic attitude that can lack authenticity. As Jim Collins wrote in *Good to Great*, "You must maintain unwavering faith that you can and will prevail in the end, regardless of the difficulties, AND at the same time have the discipline to confront the most brutal facts of your reality, whatever they may be."

Collins had interviewed Admiral James Stockdale, a former vice-presidential running mate of Ross Perot. More importantly, Stockdale had been one of the longest-held captives in the Vietnam War. When Collins asked Stockdale why certain people had survived their captivity while others had not, the admiral replied that the blindly optimistic prisoners of war had the greatest difficulty. They believed with such fervor that they would be released by some arbitrary date in the future that when that date came and went and they had not been freed, they had a much more difficult time than the grounded optimists, those men who believed they would get out, but who were never less than realistic about the odds they were facing.

Great salespeople are optimists rooted in the realities of their own endeavors. They know that they will not be successful every time, but they don't allow themselves to be drawn into webs of negativity and pessimism from sales failures or pessimistic colleagues. They marshal their own energy and emotion to drive themselves toward success, even while accepting that the odds will not always be in their favor. They use disappointment as a learning opportunity to improve their next customer interaction, and they know that there are few jobs, customers, or situations that won't have some setbacks along the way.

Watching Top Performers

"Who's the Elvis?"

—BONO

If you want to become a better salesperson, here's an idea: Find a great salesperson and study her. Notice her body language. Listen to her greeting. Learn from her closing techniques. What I suspect you will discover is that she has a passion for what she does, that she believes that the customer is better off for having worked with her. What you will likely discover is that she listens well and she speaks with an assertiveness that instills confidence in her customer. She is, by all accounts, connecting on an emotional level.

Grab your phone, open your notes app, and make a few observations. Watch for things that salesperson does consistently as she works with her customers. I expect that you will see a pattern of behavior that repeats itself again and again, even on those occasions when she is not successful in closing the sale. She has a game plan, and it always includes a commitment to really connecting with her customers.

Greg McMahon is a top performer. He's just one of those guys who appears to have been born to sell and, as good as he is at doing it, he seems to derive even more pleasure from coaching his colleagues. He has long preached to his teammates about the dangers of selling on dry facts and product information alone, preferring to extol the merits of connecting emotionally with clients. One of the training exercises Greg used in the store was to challenge the team to imagine that they were selling an engagement ring to a blind person. He believed that if they could learn to listen really well, and then to paint pictures for the client, they would be far less likely to resort to a litany of tired and uninspiring product facts and irrelevant details. Greg said that the game of selling a diamond, and, I suppose, just about anything else, would change dramatically when the security blanket of color, clarity, carat weight, etc. was taken away.

One day, Greg was challenged to walk his talk when a couple came in to purchase an engagement ring. The two women appeared to be in their midforties and midthirties respectively, and the younger of them was blind. Her partner was holding her arm, and the couple displayed all the excitement and nervousness you would expect as they sought help in finding their perfect ring. Greg confessed that he experienced a brief moment of anxiety as he approached the nervous couple, and he knew that he would now have to put into practice what he had long preached.

He introduced himself to the two women and then led them to the diamond room where they all took a seat. After offering them a beverage, Greg learned the blind woman, Sarah, was a drug counselor for the state. He asked about whether being sight impaired was a hindrance in the job, and she replied, "Not at all. I can tell far more from their tone of voice than I ever could from seeing what they look like." Greg had come into the conversation wondering how he was going to handle the challenge of selling an engagement ring to a blind person, and she was already telling him how to do it. Furthermore, Sarah's feedback was reinforcing Greg's philosophy about selling; the conversation had quickly shaped itself into an emotional connection. He was being reminded that his tone of voice—and not just what he had to say—was going to be very important throughout the conversation.

Greg was very attentive to the visual clues Sarah gave him as she held and examined the rings he presented. He also watched her partner, Mary, very closely, and he noticed how much was being communicated between the two women, even without words. He took his cues from Sarah's facial expressions and from how Mary would gently touch her hand when she liked something. Leonard Mlodinow wrote in *Subliminal: How Your Unconscious Mind Rules Your Behavior*:

> The pitch, timbre, volume, and cadence of your voice, the speed with which you speak, and even the way you modulate pitch and volume, are all hugely influential factors in how convincing you are, and how people judge your state of mind and your character.

The experience was a remarkable gift for Greg. Everything he had preached, from listening intently, to his open-ended and sincere questioning, to his tone of voice, was put into practice with Mary and Sarah. Without ever mentioning diamond carat weight, color, or clarity, typical conversation topics when discussing diamonds, the sale was made, and the happy couple left the store delighted with their experience and their ring. Greg told me that he made two new friends and that Mary and Sarah come into the store now and again to catch up with him.

I have no doubt that this story has been told countless numbers of times in his store. It represents a fantastic opportunity for the salespeople who witnessed the experience firsthand, or who heard about it afterward, to comprehend the value of making a meaningful emotional connection with your customer. It was a powerful reminder of the value of observing the many visual cues that are communicated from customers, and of the great importance we ought to place on our tone of voice when engaging customers.

Greg is, and always has been, a stellar sales performer. His wiring and his drive ensure that he will always be a very effective salesperson. His immense value as a sales producer may only be exceeded by the example he sets daily for the salespeople who have the good sense to watch and emulate his great work.

Greeting

"Vision is the most dominant human sense."

—Connie Dieken

I have noticed an emerging and quite bewildering trend in recent months. For some reason, a number of seemingly disconnected businesses have adopted a greeting that is as impersonal as it is nonsensical.

At the Wyndham New Yorker Hotel, the Row Hotel, Au Bon Pain, and Duane Reade stores, the employees at the reception desks and check-out counters are greeting customers with "The following guest." It's hard to imagine why anyone would think that this was an appropriate way to greet customers and guests, but someone, bewildering as it is to me, was somehow able to sell that ridiculous idea to the aforementioned retail stores and hotels.

Instead of looking to the next customer in line, or to the next guest at the check-in desk, and greeting them with a warm smile and a sincere welcome, I watched jaded clerks in these establishments utter that inane summons without raising their eyes to look at the customers or guests, and all without a modicum of warmth. Despite the best intentions of some corporate wizard, it is entirely possible that the employees of those respective companies were actually being conditioned to sound and act in a very impersonal way by the greeting itself.

Rather than focus on the specific words used in greeting a customer, we ought to be much more interested in what kind of nonverbal cues we are communicating. According to Todorov and Willis at Princeton, it takes one-tenth of one second to establish a bias (positive or negative) when we meet someone. Once we understand that, it should become patently obvious that our body language, immediately apparent and directly communicative, is what is most important. We can say anything we want to say, we can repeat verbatim whatever the latest corporate mandate is, but we will not make a human connection if our body language communicates that we would really rather be someplace else. What we show the customer in being open and welcoming, and particularly in how we look at them, with good and sincere eye contact, is tremendously important. Sanjida O'Connell wrote in *Mindreading: An Investigation into How We Learn to Love and Lie*:

> Eyes are terribly important, they convey a wealth of emotion. Think of the old silent films: even without words they are easily understood. Charlie Chaplin was one of the first people to use close-ups in cinema. He deliberately decided to employ this novel camera technique because he wanted people to see the emotion in his face and knew that they could understand what he was thinking by seeing his expression.

I was asked during a speaking engagement in California last year what I felt an appropriate greeting was when a customer first enters the store. The question was asked by someone I would describe as a very thoughtful and engaged retailer. The fact that she was asking what should be a very rudimentary question speaks volumes to the lack of clarity or consensus on the matter. So, if it's not "The following guest," what is it? For an answer, I'll give a nod to the Supreme Court in 1964, when Justice Potter Stewart wrote of pornography that while he might not be able to describe it, he would nonetheless know it when he saw it.

I recently went to Nordstrom. It would be hard to describe exactly what the salespeople's approach was, but I know it felt awfully right to me. I was greeted in a low-key but attentive way, and every salesperson I passed made a point of making eye contact and saying hello. I felt no pressure, and I was not aware of any stalkers watching me from behind clothing racks. I was ever mindful that there were available salespeople should I need them, but that I was welcome to peruse the clothing at my leisure until I needed to engage a salesperson. I walked out of the store that day proudly carrying a Nordstrom bag, and I never felt better about a shopping experience. I couldn't tell you what specific greeting or words were used, but there was no doubt that the nonverbal cues were very positive and sincere, and that is what was communicated to me.

Contrast that experience with one I had at another national retail chain, where I had occasion to visit multiple stores in the same day. Each store I visited greeted me exactly the same way, and the entire process—from how I was welcomed, to being offered water or cappuccino, to being turned over to another salesperson—was brilliantly consistent, a testament to the clarity of their internal communication and to their training department. The problem, however, was that none of it felt authentic. To be fair to the company, how many customers are likely to visit more than one of their stores in a given day and, as a consequence, recognize the to-the-letter consistency of each greeting? That said, it never felt less than forced and insincere, as though the salespeople were going through the motions. In many respects, the form and programmed nature of the routine was not a lot different than "The following guest." It wasn't about me or any other individual customer, it was a series of human beings acting in sequence like they were programmed robots. The whole experience left me aching for a real human connection.

The next time you are in a zoo or an aquarium, watch the people around you. Pay particular attention to how they react when an animal appears to lunge at them. Despite the fact that the potential attacker is behind bars or reinforced glass, it is amazing how often we jump back or flinch when we believe we are in danger. Cognitively, of course, we know that the animals present no danger to us. They are firmly ensconced behind whatever barrier the zoo has erected to keep us safe while allowing us to get up close. Nonetheless, our first instinct is to flinch, or even run, when we perceive danger.

Those instincts are genetic, and they are hardwired. Within seconds, of course, we are able to laugh at ourselves as we quickly rationalize that we are not in any danger. That cognitive rationale, however, comes only after the very visceral and immediate reaction that made us flinch or run from the cage or barrier. We can say whatever we want to the customer when they enter our stores, but their first instinct will always be to react to what you communicate long before a word is ever spoken. The warmth of your smile, the welcoming look in your eyes, the manner in which you shape your body language will always take precedence over the words you use. Dennis Postema wrote in *Psychology of Sales*: "Every first approach toward a customer should be relaxed, easy, and friendly. Never walk up behind a customer. Make certain to always come from a sideways or front-facing entry point."

Postema's counsel and the Nordstrom culture of warm acknowledgement, at a respectful distance, feels just right to me. Clearly, if a customer walks into a store and approaches a salesperson with a question, the greeting can be more direct and the engagement more immediate. Otherwise, a sincere greeting, such as "Good morning" or "Good afternoon," a warm smile, and a little breathing room strikes just the right chord as far as I'm concerned.

Communicate Assertively

"Wise men speak because they have something to say;
fools because they have to say something."

—PLATO

I am not a mind reader, nor have I ever been a mind reader, and I am fairly certain that if you gave me the option of becoming a telepath, I would politely decline your offer. You might give me a multitude of reasons as to why someone would want to become a psychic, but I am quite sure (of course, not being a mind reader, I can't be *absolutely* sure) that I would still decline your offer.

Can you imagine how bad it might feel if, upon meeting someone, you were to discover that you reminded them of a teacher or former boss with whom they had a very stressful relationship? What if you brought back memories of a particularly harrowing personal relationship with a former boyfriend or girlfriend? Do I need to carry that load? I think not.

How would you feel if, upon sitting down for an interview, you discovered that the interviewer has already concluded there is no way she is hiring you for the position? We learned in the last chapter that people form biases within one-tenth of one second of meeting someone. Thank you very much, but I'll pass on knowing that stuff.

I am happy to not be able to read your mind, but I reserve the right to closely observe your body language and to listen very intently to what you are saying so that I can understand what is going on, and I want my salesperson to do the same thing.

I want him or her to take charge and, quite frankly, to communicate with me in a clear, confident, and assertive manner. I don't want there to be any attempt to read my mind, just ask me good probing, open-ended questions and listen, really listen, to what I am telling you. I may not be able to articulate with absolute clarity what my needs are, but I'll give you a few clues and, through your deductive-reasoning skills and your drive, you ought to be able to help me figure out what my needs are.

There's a small boutique hotel that I stay at in New York on a regular basis. Every single time I walk into the lobby, I am greeted with a warm smile by the guy or gal behind the check-in desk, and they always ask me the same question: "How can I help you?" It's hard to get too mad at them, as they usually look happy to see me, but here's a clue: I am walking into the lobby of your hotel pulling my luggage behind me. So let me ask the question: How DO you think you can help me? How about making a reasonable deduction that I must be checking in!

I know that assumptions are dangerous—and I might actually be coming into your hotel looking for directions—but if you were to play the odds and determine that I did indeed want to check in, and if you were to greet me with that same welcoming smile and say, "Welcome back, sir, it's nice to see you again!" what could possibly go wrong? How could I get mad at you for that? Would I say, "What the heck's the matter with you? I just came in here looking for directions to Times Square!" No, probably not.

As a salesperson, take charge in an assertive and respectful manner. I really don't want to go to the barber to debate whether I need a haircut or not, and I certainly don't want to go to the doctor to diagnose my own ailment. If I have taken the trouble to visit your place of business, there's a pretty good certainty that I want you to take care of my needs.

So assert yourself and lead the process. Asking open-ended questions such as "Tell me about some of the things you have bought for her in the past?" can be very effective. How about, "How would you describe her personal style?" "What are her favorite colors?"

Whatever you do, please do not product-dump on me. Don't start throwing stuff at the wall hoping that something will stick—that doesn't help me at all. Please don't use me as a sounding board to demonstrate your amazing product knowledge. I'll ask you for product details if it is important, but please don't consume my precious time with information that is irrelevant to me.

Take charge. Tell me that you will be delighted to take care of my needs, and demonstrate in your words, your demeanor, and your actions that you respect my time and that you will help to satisfy my needs. Repeat some of the key points back to me so that I know you are listening, and don't be afraid to ask for clarification when needed.

I am not a mind reader, and I don't expect you to be one, either. There's a reason I walked into your place of business and, unlike my friends at the hotel in New York, go ahead and make the assumption that I am there to do business with you. Welcome me, engage me, ask me great questions, listen to me, and when you are confident that we have arrived at a good solution, go ahead and ask me for the sale.

Open-ended Questions

Asking open-ended questions is a great way to get the customer talking. Getting the customer talking is the best way to establish a connection, and establishing a connection is the first stop on the path to making a sale. What else needs to be said? Adam Grant wrote in *Give and Take*:

> By asking people questions about their plans and intentions, we increase the likelihood that they actually act on these plans and intentions. Research shows that if I ask you whether you're planning to buy a new computer in the next six months, you'll be 18 percent more likely to go out and buy one.

When you consider what it is possible to do with only twenty-six letters, it is just mind-numbing. I marvel every time Stephen King comes out with a new book. He's working his way up to a billion-page book, and the dude gets it done with the same twenty-six letters that the rest of us have to work so hard to shape into something of value.

Here's my challenge to you: take those twenty-six letters and fashion them into a select few questions that can get a customer talking when he or she enters your store. Banish "How can I help you today?" and replace it with an appropriate greeting such as "Good morning" or "Good afternoon."

If you accept that we are much more likely to be engaged when we share stories, it follows that asking open-ended questions can be a great vehicle to getting the customer to deliver a mini-story, in his own words. So go ahead and ask some open-ended questions, do not lead or interrupt the customer as he answers, listen very intently to his words, and closely observe his body language.

On the phone yesterday, a manager at my favorite auto-repair shop listened to my tale of woe about a perceived grievance we had. Throughout the call, he never interrupted, but he would occasionally pepper the conversation with questions such as "Tell me why you feel that way" or "I'm sorry you feel that way. Can you give me an example?" By the end of the conversation, I was almost rooting for him, and not surprisingly we were able to come to a mutually satisfying resolution.

There are many open-ended questions that can be used to get a customer talking, but some examples might include:

"Tell me about the person you are buying this for."
"What is most important to you with this purchase?"
"How would you describe her particular style?"
"Tell me about some of the gifts that have worked well in the past."

While there are few absolutes when it comes to language, asking open-ended questions is, quite frankly, a much better way to engage a customer than asking yes-or-no questions. Consider the following:

"Is this for your wife?" (Yes/No)
"Is this a birthday gift?" (Yes/No)
"Have you ever bought her a pendant?" (Yes/No)
"Do you like this?" (Yes/No)

The flip side of asking open-ending questions is lazily defaulting to yes-or-no questions that can be quickly dismissed, consciously or unconsciously, by a customer. He or she may not intend to be dismissive, but when you walk someone down that blind alley, you will occasionally hit a brick wall.

Pat Henneberry, a very good trainer in her own right, shared some questions that she uses when she is selling engagement rings to a guy. She'll ask, "If you were to buy a brand-new house, describe for me the kind of furniture you think she would buy for the house." This question enables the customer to psychologically and, perhaps unconsciously, assume ownership in the process of understanding what might be important to his fiancée.

Pat will also ask him to describe the kinds of things she likes to do when they go on vacation together. Again, getting the customer engaged in the process of discovery can be very helpful on any number of levels.

Great open-ended questions enable you to practice your most important trait, listening. The more you listen, the more you will learn. You will likely tap into a much richer variety of responses and, if you don't lead the customer with your own biases, you may find yourselves in a very special place that enriches the entire customer experience and results in a sale. And, lest we still need reminding, that's why we do what we do in the first place.

Listening

"The most important thing I look for in a musician is
whether he knows how to listen."

—Duke Ellington

Even as I write the words *practice listening*, I am cringing in the knowledge that it is a very difficult thing to do. I know what you're thinking: How difficult could it possibly be to just *shut the heck up and listen* to what the customer has to say? Well, as it happens, it is an exceedingly difficult thing to do because listening involves more than just shutting the heck up. As Daniel Goleman wrote in *Emotional Intelligence*: "People's emotions are rarely put into words, far more often they are expressed through other cues. The key to intuiting another's feelings is in the ability to read nonverbal channels; tone of voice, gesture, facial expression, and the like."

If you are blessed with good reserves of empathy, and you are wired to listen well to what is being said and what is not being said, and to recognize the myriad cues being communicated through the customer's body language and nonverbally, you already understand the importance of listening. You have been practicing listening all of your life, and you probably couldn't imagine a scenario when you weren't in tune to the verbal and nonverbal cues from your friends and family, your classmates and teachers, and, ultimately, your customers. If, on the other hand, you are not a skilled listener, you will be at a considerable disadvantage in trying to decipher what the customers' real needs are.

It has been said that it is impossible to be objective about oneself, and knowing whether you are a good listener or not is a good an example of that. In many respects, that dilemma is all the more pronounced in a sales environment, where we must contend with the myth that the silver-tongued salesperson always gets the sale. This is absolutely not the case, and, unfortunately, that perception feeds the stereotype too often associated with used-car salesmen.

Great salespeople are always good listeners. They understand the importance of hearing and reading what their customers are communicating, even when the customer herself may not be entirely sure of what her needs are. She may or may not have a general idea of what she might like to buy for a particular occasion, so the subtle cues that Goleman referred to provide a rich vein of information if you look closely enough for it.

With or without the inherent wiring to be empathic and to listen with purpose, you must be ever-cognizant of this fundamentally important trait. If it does not come easily to you, read what you can on the subject and ask your colleagues to tell you when they notice you are not as present as you might have been with a customer or, for that matter, with a coworker. Greenberg and Sweeney's *How to Hire and Develop Your Next Top Performer* does a great job speaking to the power of good listening. You might even consider occasionally asking a colleague to subtly film you as you work with a customer so that you can review the video afterward to see if you look engaged and if you appear to be actively listening.

Active listening means that you are fully present with the customer; you are not allowing yourself to become easily distracted; you are not listening for the sole purpose of deciding what it is you want to say. Active listening means that you are, to quote Goleman, "intuiting" what the customer is communicating. It may be that the customer has a clear sense of what she wants—and that is being communicated with verbal and/or nonverbal cues. It may also be true that the customer is communicating that she is not really sure about what she wants, but she can't or won't say that. She may need your help to excavate those things that are most important to her as she seeks a satisfactory solution to her needs.

Here's a typical disconnect that happens in retail stores. A salesperson is showing a piece of merchandise to a customer, and when the salesperson asks the customer if he likes it, he responds by telling her that he does. However, instead of focusing on the item she is holding, his attention is drawn elsewhere, as he continues to search the store for some elusive prize, or a moment of divine inspiration. What the customer could be communicating, without actually saying so, is that the price is too high, or too low, or that the piece just isn't what he wants—even if he can't specifically articulate what it is he does want. Barry Schwartz writes in *The Paradox of Choice*: "When people are asked to give reasons for their preferences, they may struggle to find the words. Sometimes aspects of their reaction that are not the most important determinants of their overall feelings are nonetheless easier to verbalize."

An astute salesperson will pick up on the customer's body language and continue to ask open-ended questions. Questions such as, "It seems to me that you like this ring, but that there's something not exactly right about it. Tell me what you like, and tell me what doesn't work for you with this particular item." All too often the salesperson stands there, not quite knowing what to do next, having backed herself into a corner by not asking better questions and by not really listening to the customer. We then see an uncomfortable little shuffle (for the customer and the salesperson) and a prolonged silence or, worse still, a product-information dump, as the salesperson tries in vain to convince the customer that this is the right choice by spewing an avalanche of irrelevant facts.

Lara Lambrecht has a stellar record of great retail-sales performance in a number of different stores. She shared the following story with me:

I was working in the store one day when a good-looking man walked in. As I approached him, I noticed that there was something about his walk that seemed oddly disconnected from his tanned complexion and his elegant attire. I welcomed him to the store, and I tried one of my usual connector lines, complimenting his tan and contrasting it with my own whiter-than-white complexion.

That approach is usually enough to get a smile and a little connection with most customers, and to put them at ease, but there was something different about this particular customer, and getting him to be at ease was going to be more work than is usual. I kept a warm smile on my face and found myself descending uncomfortably into one of the more awkward and unsettling starts to a customer conversation in my twenty years in sales.

Most people who visit our store do so with the aim of buying an engagement ring, surprising a loved one with an amazing piece of jewelry, or picking out something to mark a special relationship or occasion. In this situation, while all the elements of sparkling diamonds gleaming countertops and occasion lighting were in place, his demeanor and countenance seemed eerily at odds with the environment; he looked very sad, almost forlorn. Since he was not making conversation or eye contact with me, I gave him a little space to circle the showroom before approaching him again.

"It looks like you've just flown in from someplace wonderful! Your tan is amazing! Tell me all about it!"

It was a risk, but I had to get him to open up.

He reluctantly made eye contact with me and said that he and his wife had just returned from Jamaica.

Ah ha, common ground at last, I thought! I told him that I loved it there, but he still looked like he was incredibly distracted and maybe even a little depressed.

I continued to try and connect with him, taking a more direct approach and pulling pieces from the cases. I even tried a silly joke or two. Finally, I said, "I feel like you are on a mission. Let me help. What are we looking for?" I then proceeded to sit down, and I invited him to take a seat. He said he was looking for an engagement ring to replace his wife's. Their trip to Jamaica had been an anniversary vacation, and they had inadvertently left all of their jewelry at home. When they returned, their best friend met them at the airport, and he broke the devastating news that their house had burned to the ground.

The friend had been checking in on their bulldog several times a day, and sleeping there overnight, but the fire started in his absence and their beloved bulldog had tragically perished. That, he said, was the biggest blow.

The news was, understandably, a stunner to me, and it took me a few moments to regain my composure. I had been trying to engage him with trivial humor and petty throwaway lines, not knowing the depth of his grief and loss.

He started to tear up, and I did, too (my rule: no one cries alone). I took the reins and told him we were going to find his wife something amazing. We'd find a new ring to dazzle her and to craft a whole new set of memories. He visibly brightened and we found a spectacular round brilliant-cut diamond, a departure from her original emerald-cut diamond. We then found a setting that wowed him, and he began to nod his head with excitement as a reluctant smile crossed his face for the first time since he entered the store.

He then told me that his wife was celebrating an important birthday the next day.

"How long will she have to wait for it?" he asked.

I told him to come back in an hour and a half, and then I leveraged all the goodwill I had amassed with our jeweler (tears still in my eyes) to make sure that we could deliver the ring in time.

He left the store, a little lighter than when he first came in, promising to return to pick up the ring in a little while. It was then that I began to imagine what it might feel like to lose my dog in such tragic circumstances. I would, of course, be absolutely devastated. I wouldn't want a replacement, but I wouldn't turn away a puppy I could hug and that could help with my family's grieving.

I went online and found a local breeder with a litter of French bulldog puppies ready for sale a mere fifteen minutes from our store.

When he returned, I showed him the gorgeous diamond ring, all ready to be presented to his wife. While it was being wrapped, I gave him pictures of the French bulldog puppies I found and a map to the breeder's house. I told him the breeder was expecting him. He really smiled then, a broad and grateful smile that lit up his face . . . and we both cried again.

I have had much bigger and more lucrative sales in my career but never anything as satisfying as that sale. We get to impact people's lives in ways that most people can't begin to imagine. We just have to care enough to really listen to what is going on with our customers, and sometimes that takes real work.

There is, quite frankly, no substitute for purposeful listening. That means more than just staying quiet while you plot your next move. It means being completely present with the customer, tuning out all unnecessary distractions, and paying attention to the spoken words, the unspoken words, and the customer's body language. Lara's story is remarkable for so many reasons, but her compassion, her empathy, and her decency turned a terribly sad situation and a very challenging exchange into a beautiful connection with a lovely conclusion, given the circumstances.

Even if you are a good listener, it is always a good idea to continue to work at sharpening your instincts. You can do that by continually checking yourself, and by asking colleagues to do likewise. There are numerous books and online resources that address the topic of empathy, and YouTube is a great source of material from TED Talks and elsewhere. I also find Twitter to be an amazing source of information if you take the time to follow the many great sources of information.

Using Humor

"It ain't the heat, it's the humility."

—YOGI BERRA

Your first objective when a customer visits your store is to make an emotional connection with him or her. This essential human need is generally understood by most, but not always easily accomplished. To test that sentiment, walk into a few retail stores the next time you are in your local mall or shopping plaza. You are likely to find a myriad of different reactions—some better than others—but I suspect that when you find a salesperson who is striving to connect with you, she might be the exception more than the rule. It obviously won't happen from the typical "Can I help you?" or the all-too-frequent indifference that you are even in the store. Who was it who once said that retail would be great if it weren't for the darn customers? Why is it that so many salespeople seem to live by that sentiment?

One of the best ways to engage people is to use humor. Having said that, trying to explain humor to someone is a little bit like chewing their food for them. It just doesn't work. You either get it, or you don't. Or, to put it more aptly, you either have it or you don't. Rod Martin reported in his book *The Psychology of Humor* that 94 percent of people surveyed believed they have an above-average sense of humor. Seriously! The remaining 6 percent apparently have a lot to answer for.

To be fair, I think that we all have the capacity to enjoy humor when we see it in everyday situations, and we generally recognize how effective it can be as a human connector. Just watch how people respond when there is a humorous anecdote being shared. The body language of the listener changes completely as they listen to the story, which allows them to be led wherever the storyteller wants to take them. Humor is captivating, and laughter is contagious.

When I think back on all of the people I have worked with in my career, I find, like most people, that I am drawn to people who have a sense of humor. There's the brilliantly quick wit of Adam, Johnny Mc's dry wit, Russo's hilarious body and facial contortions, and Shawn's down-home quirkiness ("Shut the front door"). We all love to laugh. It's a great gift of the human condition, and it can mask a great many sins if we allow it to.

If you've ever wondered about the power of laughter, listen intently to the comments from people around you on an airplane when you hit some particularly bad turbulence. I'm not sure if I'm one of those people or not (when I was younger, I used to take the hour-long flight from Dublin to London in a state of paralytic fear), but some people use humor and laughter to deal with stress when an event outside of their control seems to threaten their safety. I'm never quite sure in those situations if I'm glad to have the jesters aboard, or if I just want them to shut up so that I can pray quietly.

Besides serving as a diversion from a near-death experience, humor serves a good many masters, and it can be very helpful in a retail sales environment when used appropriately and authentically. It can serve as a catalyst to help connect strangers when they first meet—a particularly useful tool in the world of sales. Humor can also diffuse or alleviate tension from a potentially difficult situation with a customer or a coworker, enabling both parties to move beyond a potentially difficult interaction.

Sales is a serious business. It comes with a great many demands and pressures, and retail in particular seems to be filled with peaks and valleys, as the pressure of producing sales amps up in the busier times and the stress of finding business increases during the quieter periods. Both the former and the latter scenarios can be helped greatly with a little well-placed humor. Laughter releases endorphins and dopamine in our brains, which helps to make us feel more energized and more optimistic—particularly good tools in a retail environment. Laughter can also heighten our creativity and help with self-esteem—also not such a bad thing in a sales environment, where rejection is an ever-present companion.

Steer clear of humor that is off-color or might offend people (that used to mean no religion, race, or politics), but find ways to see the humor in situations and share that humor in an authentic way. Your customers' mirror neurons will fire in response to your humor and authenticity, and a warm connection will have been established between you and the customer. In an earlier chapter, we heard how Lara Lambrecht attempted to use humor to connect with what appeared to be a very challenging customer. Thankfully, her empathy kept her from coming across as insensitive in a situation with deeper undertones than she could ever have imagined.

Shaina Williams, who manages a retail store in the Denver area, shared the following anecdote with me:

A few of our Million-Dollar Club sales consultants have a really good sense of humor. One simple but very memorable example has stayed with me and brings a smile to my face whenever I think of it. A gentleman walked into our store one afternoon and began to hover over our Rolex case. One of our consultants worked with him, and after a few minutes he decided to buy the watch for himself. As delighted as he was, he nervously suggested that he was just a little worried about what his wife's response would be when he arrived home with his new bauble.

As we began to process the sale and pull the paperwork together, another one of our sales consultants, who had overheard the conversation, walked over to him with a thirty-five-thousand-dollar Canary diamond ring and humorously suggested, "You know, this watch thing would go over a lot smoother if you were to bring a little something home for her."

The customer laughed the laugh of someone who had just been given a get-out-of-jail-free card and, much to our amazement, he replied, "You're right." And he bought the ring, too. He actually thanked us for the idea ("Say, here's a little $35,000 something to throw in the bag") and he bounced out of our store, delighted with his new watch and the thought of presenting the beautiful ring to his wife. All because one of our sales consultants had a good sense of humor and the confidence to use it with him.

What is very interesting to me about Shaina's story is not just the idea that humor served as a catalyst to create retail magic but that in the process of making an important sale (when many salespeople get the jitters in case something might go wrong), one of the salespeople had the confidence to explore whether there might be an opportunity for an important add-on sale. Couching that exploration in humor gave both the salesperson and the customer an out if the suggestion was unwelcome. It would, quite frankly, have been difficult for the customer to take offense given the nature of the approach. Robin Sharma wrote in *The Leader Who Had No Title*:

> Most of us think words need to be so serious. We're afraid that if we laugh and have some fun and get a bit playful at the right time, we'll be perceived as wasting time and being unproductive. But here's the truth, my friend: having fun while you do great work will help you boost productivity. Fun makes you more engaged in whatever you are doing. Fun makes you want to collaborate more. And when people are having fun, the energy of the entire organization shifts into higher and higher levels.

Or, as the comedian Billy Connolly once asked, "Who discovered we could get milk from cows, and what did he think he was doing at the time?"

Telling Stories

"Like all people who try to exhaust a subject, he
exhausted his listeners."

—Oscar Wilde

I read a story recently in JCK Online that quoted the Tiffany & Co. CEO Frederic Cumenal, who said, "We want (sales associates) to be stronger in storytelling, having a better ability to deliver messages about our heritage." When I read Cumenal's comments, I was reminded of one of the first sales I ever made at Tiffany & Co., a Breguet watch, and I am as certain now as I was then that one of the main reasons the customer bought the watch was because I told him that Napoleon Bonaparte once owned a Breguet. I remember the customer's demeanor completely transforming when he learned that the French general once owned the brand. It was his chance to be connected to a major historical figure and a part of history, and he was clearly excited by that.

That was in 1986, and the fact that we are still extolling the benefits of storytelling is a testament to its transformative power—taking seemingly inanimate and even technical objects and transforming them into incredibly aspirational objets d'art. It is also telling that the head of Tiffany & Co., a successful retailer that has managed to infuse its message with stories and emotions, still feels the need to promote the necessity of storytelling as an important initiative in these times.

Advances in neuroimaging in recent years now allow us to see and measure the effects of customer engagement. Using fMRI machines, which measure brain activity, we can now see firsthand what happens when a customer responds, negatively or positively, to various stimuli. This engagement is very telling, and it does not always align with what the customer might be telling you or, in fact, what the customer *thinks* he or she believes. Lewis and Dart wrote in *The New Rules of Retail*:

> So how do we think the business model of neuroconnectivity works? The business model is designed to drive the entire experience of three things: the dopamine rush in anticipation of shopping, compelling the customer to visit the store; the joy of the actual shopping experience itself; and the final satisfaction of consuming or using the product or service. This is the neurological connection with the customer on all conscious and subconscious levels.

There is no better way to ignite neuroconnectivity than to tell meaningful stories, particularly when the customer's need is tied to a person and/or an occasion that is important to them. Storytelling is an art form, and it is an immensely effective way to create an emotional bond with a customer. Good stories draw the customer in and serve as a catalyst to communicate passion and sincerity about your company, your products, and your services. More importantly, they also communicate a desire to emotionally connect with your customer and to help him or her fulfill their needs. A diatribe of facts and figures about products or services should never be confused with storytelling.

While you can weave information about features and benefits into your stories, a laundry lists of dry facts is a great way to disengage a customer and default to a wholly unfulfilling conversation that lives in and around a commodity discussion, lacking passion and engagement. Connie Dieken wrote in *Talk Less, Say More*: "Don't get bogged down in excess details. Your story is a means to the end, not the end itself. Share enough specifics to ignite imaginations, but not so many that your listeners get lost in irrelevant details."

Good storytelling can influence and inspire consumer behavior, and, in sales, it should lead to purchasing decisions being made. However, we ought not to confuse *talking* with storytelling. There are far more salespeople who can talk and talk, filling space with inane and irrelevant rhetoric without moving the sales process forward. You will only interest your customer if you are able to emotionally engage them with relevant stories. What you deem to be relevant and what they deem to be relevant must align, and storytelling should lead to a sale.

My colleague and I were visiting one of our customers in Dallas, Texas, last year. We were very glad for the air conditioning and the warm welcome, and as we settled into the comfortable seating in the sales office, one of the salespeople approached us and began, a tad sheepishly, to make a request of us. She was wondering, almost apologizing as she was asking, if there was any possibility of us making a particular ring extra fast for her. We asked her what she had in mind and when she needed it. She explained what she wanted and then she finally let spill that she needed the ring for the weekend, that upcoming weekend. It was, I should point out, Wednesday, which meant we had to make the ring immediately and get it to her without any delay.

Fast-forward to Friday, just two days later, and she called our office to exclaim her amazement at the fact that we had delivered the ring and the quality was, as she said, wonderful. However (insert *Jaws* theme music here), the finger size was wrong. Our response was to remake the ring that very day and send it overnight so that she had it on Saturday in time for her customer appointment. To put that into perspective, a more typical delivery time for that kind of thing is anywhere from four to six weeks. To say the customer was impressed would be an understatement.

Telling your customers you have fast delivery could never in a million years convey the message the same way as simply telling the above story. We can all relate to storytelling as long as it is relevant and believable. We could have said, "We have lightning-fast delivery," and, true as it may be, it might have sounded like its boastful and evil step-sister, "Nine out of ten doctors approve of this product."

Peter Guber wrote in *Tell to Win*, "Whatever story you tell, if you are perceived to be authentic, your audience will hear you empathetically and be more likely to embrace your passion." If you are even border-line awake in retail sales, you ought to be accumulating scores of great stories that can be used as needed. Engaged salespeople are part of a daily production that delivers great experiences to customers, and those interactions very often deliver wonderful stories and anecdotes. Those stories should be used to engage and inspire your customers and, to borrow from Guber, they should be authentic. If a story or experience moved you, then share it. Your passion and honesty in telling that story will influence and inspire the customer far more than rattling off a boring list of product attributes.

Emotional Connection

"When you fish for love, bait with your heart, not your brain."

—MARK TWAIN

David Lewis wrote in his book *Impulse*: "We all like to regard ourselves as rational human beings. To believe we act only after careful reflection and thoughtful deliberation. The fact is, however, that our actions are *mindless* far more often than they are *mindful*: the product not of logic and reason but of habits driven by emotions."

If this was the Wild West, this is the point where all the retailer cowboys and cowgirls would throw their hats in the air and shoot their guns skyward to celebrate the fact that it's not all about the facts. If it were—all about the facts, that is— why would we need brick-and-mortar stores? We could simply shop online to our heart's content, any time of day or night, in any attire of our choosing, no engagement, emotion, or human connection necessary.

Great salespeople are not successful because they know more stuff than their colleagues. They are not successful because they strong-arm their customers into submission, and, listen closely now, they are not more successful because they are *luckier* than their less celebrated coworkers. They are successful because they understand how to emotionally connect with their customers to create meaningful experiences that transcend mere product information.

As a point of clarification, I am not saying that product knowledge is a bad thing, but we must choose to connect on a level that is more about *feelings* and less about *information-dumping*. As Sheena Iyengar wrote in *The Art of Choosing*, "We tend to have a better memory for things that excite our senses than for straight facts and dry statistics."

My wife and I went to see a concert some time ago in a lovely theater here in Massachusetts. The concert was a tribute to Frank Sinatra and Ella Fitzgerald, and it featured many of the songs that we've all come to love over the years such as "Fly Me to The Moon," "The Way You Look Tonight," and "My Funny Valentine."

As you might expect, the show featured two singers, a man (the Sinatra guy) and a woman (playing Ella) and a really great, swinging band. The drummer and upright bass player were joined by a three-piece brass section and a very accomplished keyboard player. In a nutshell, the band was great and the singers were, well . . . a major disappointment.

When I attend shows that feature vocalists, I try to suppress any desire to overly, or unfairly, focus on the singers. I sing myself—I have done so for many years—and I am particularly sensitive to interpretations of songs from *The Great American Songbook*, as I have a great love for that genre. Despite, or perhaps because of, the great band, I simply could not ignore these uninspiring performances by "Ella" and "Frank." They had, at best, a rather tenuous relationship with the lyrics, and if either of them had any great feeling for the songs, it certainly didn't translate to where we were sitting, six or seven rows from the stage.

When I woke up the following morning, and my mind returned to the show, I found myself thinking about what an interesting metaphor that show was for many retail environments. I wondered if there were great "swinging" stores that were being let down by underperforming salespeople, who might also have a somewhat tenuous relationship with the lyrics and a questionable emotional connection in their daily performance. Have you ever experienced a salesperson who seems to be saying the right things and yet he or she somehow manages to sound inauthentic?

Stephen Cannon, the president and CEO of Mercedes-Benz, said: "We strive to tailor the experience we deliver to exceed their expectations. That means that every interaction with our brand—whether it's our website, our showroom, our service drives, our marketing, or the phone calls they have with us—must both delight and wow them."

You can put a great band, or a great retail store, in play, but the singers must be real. They must embrace their stories in a way that is believable and that communicates to the audience, to the customer, sincerity and authenticity.

There's a line in the song "The Way You Look Tonight" that goes "and that laugh that wrinkles your nose touches my foolish heart." Go ahead, touch a foolish heart, that's where the fun begins. Make sure you are making a genuine and authentic connection with your customer because you want to. Say what you mean and mean what you say. Smile because you want to transmit that good feeling to your customers and because you like how it feels when you fully engage with your customers, your colleagues, and with each experience, small and large, during the course of your day.

My daughter, Julia, went into Boston last weekend to stand in line for four hours under a blazing-hot sun. She and her friend Jenna joined hundreds other young people for the privilege of entering a pop-up store, with exactly ten other customers, for no more than nine minutes. Once inside, they could select from a grand total of twelve different items of clothing before being hurried back outside so that the next group of twelve people could be given the same once-in-a-whatever opportunity to buy.

The event had been announced on Twitter, and it was being held in twenty-one cities around the world, including Berlin, Sydney, London, and New York. The pop-up stores were the brainchild of Kanye West (yep, Mr. Kim Kardashian, Mr. Jump-up-and-Take-Taylor-Swift's-Mic-and-Demand-the-Award-Be-Given-to-Beyoncé guy), and to say that the seemingly random items of clothing were spectacular would be, well, spectacularly wrong. After her four-hour wait, Julia delighted in handing over $75 for a basic cotton T-shirt and $110 for less-than impressive (to me) sweatshirt.

There was nothing logical about what happened. Julia could not have been any more pleased than to have had the opportunity to take half of her Saturday and stand in line to buy Kanye West's "designs," and it never occurred to her that she was overpaying for the privilege. The dad part of me, of course, was astonished that she would have subjected herself to what I might reasonably describe as the indignities of the whole situation: four hours of standing in line, only twelve people at a time in the store, nine minutes to conduct business, and a total of twelve items to select from, outrageously priced. As we walked back to the car through the Boston Public Garden, I wanted to admonish Julia for her frivolous spending. I wanted to remind her how wasteful it was to spend so much money on lousy-quality materials that were likely knocked out in a sweatshop someplace for little to nothing. I wanted to tell her that she would have been much better off saving her money, or buying something of lasting value. Then the neuroscience fan in me told me to shut the hell up. She was right, and I was totally wrong.

She didn't buy a T-shirt or a sweatshirt, she bought an experience to remember. Long after the silly clothing has been deposited into the Goodwill bin, she'll still laugh about the day she went into Boston with Jenna for the Kanye West pop-up caper.

Sure, the experience had elements of celebrity, but celebrities endorse products all the time and it doesn't make thousands of young people wait four hours to spend large sums of money on very ordinary clothing. It wasn't as though Kanye West himself was appearing at any of the pop-up stores, and there were no side events—no concerts, no food, no entertainment whatsoever built around the experience. It was as basic as it could be, and it defied all sense of logic. I mean, who would participate in such nonsense? Who would put themselves through such a huge effort to overpay for underwhelming merchandise? As it happens, thousands of young people in cities all over the world were happy to do it.

Retail is not about logical decision-making. At its best, it is about creating great experiences and making emotional connections with customers. Julia didn't know what clothing would be on offer that day in Boston. She had no idea how expensive the clothing would be or how many items would be available for purchase. She wanted to be a part of the *experience*, and she was so happy with the results that she went back again the next day to accompany another friend who did not get the opportunity to go on Saturday.

If you've ever bought a souvenir on a trip, a T-shirt at a concert or sporting event, or a beautiful piece of jewelry on a cruise, you have personally experienced the power of emotional buying. Relegating the shopping experience to the corridors of logic and reason completely misses the point of why people shop. Even when we go to the grocery store to pick up some basics, we are frequently tempted to add feel-good foods to our cart that were not on our shopping list. A bag of cookies, some of that oh-so-inviting fried chicken, or some freshly baked muffins.

Shopping in brick-and-mortar stores—and some of those wacky pop-up stores, too —will never go away. The doomsday predictions that everyone would sit at home or in their office making all of their purchasing decisions online couldn't be more wrong. I buy many of the books I read on Amazon, but I picked up Patti Smith's book *M Train* last night at Barnes & Noble, and I enjoyed every minute of my experience in that store. If you still have doubts about retail as an emotional experience, let me know and I'll have Julia give you a call. Oh wait, do you text?

Product Knowledge

"The greatest obstacle to discovery is not ignorance, it is
the illusion of knowledge."

—Daniel J. Boorstin

As a customer, there is nothing worse than asking a question and getting a blank stare. I have no issue whatsoever if a salesperson has to
go find some information for me and promises to get right back to me,
but there's something downright irritating and, I might add, wholly transparent when a salesperson tries to fake it.

Do not, however, make the mistake of thinking the spoils go to those
who know the most. They don't, and they rarely ever have. Great salespeople know their products just well enough to use information as a catalyst to emotionally connect with their customers. That, as it happens, is a
fundamentally different approach than being the smartest person in the
store who just doesn't sell very much and who, if we're being very honest, frequently bores the customers out of the door and into competitors'
stores.

I was in a leather-goods store in my local mall a while back, and I was
looking for a backpack. As I examined the less-than-impressive sample, I
asked the salesperson, almost instinctively, what the store's warranty was.
Her hesitation was enough to convince me that she either didn't know

the answer to my question or there was no warranty at all. I was even less impressed when she fumbled over a less than convincing "We stand behind our products," as if it had just occurred to her that there had to be a better answer than what she had instantaneously communicated to me through her nonverbal cues.

I was convinced of two things after my brief exchange with the salesperson: they didn't have a warranty, and whatever sales training the store provided for the salespeople was sadly insufficient. There may be occasions when you can "fake it till you make it," but this was probably not the time to do it. The salesperson (and I use that word loosely in that particular instance) should have known the answer to that simple question or replied, "Great question, sir. I just started and I don't know the answer. Give me a moment, and I'll find out for you."

There are two distinct types of product information that are essential for retail sales professionals: the basics and the emotive. The basics comprise a good working knowledge of products and/or services offered by a business. It does not have to be a deep and comprehensive understanding of every question anyone could ever ask about a given item. It should, however, be a solid understanding of the main attributes of your store's products and services.

In the jewelry business, where I have spent the majority of my career, there is ample evidence that not only are the minutiae-oriented folks not very good at selling stuff, but there is actually an inverse relationship between those salespeople who are most qualified, from a product-knowledge standpoint, and the really stellar sales performers. The premium placed on knowing stuff all too often subverts the need to keep it as simple as possible so that the salespeople can focus on really engaging the customers.

Frank Cespedes, a senior lecturer at the Harvard Business School, wrote in his book *Aligning Strategy and Sales*, "The first task of training is to build relevant competence." *Relevant* is the operative word in that statement, and that is where many weaker salespeople fall short. They believe that more information, more details, more product specifications, necessarily increases a prospect's likelihood of making a purchase. Not only is that expectation patently false, but such product information over-load has virtually no consistent correlation with sales success.

As with my backpack friend, a wing and a prayer is not a good strat-egy for customer engagement. There is perhaps no quicker way to alien-ate a prospect than by bluffing your way through his or her questions about a given product. You must know the fundamentals of the products your store carries before you can hope to move on to the stuff that really matters—emotional engagement. That said, practicing your open-ended questions, your ability to overcome objections, and your closing tech-niques is every bit as important. Product information should be dished out in small, digestible bites, and only as necessary.

The second aspect of product knowledge is very personal and very effective. Great salespeople make a habit of falling in love with certain products in their stores, and they then use those products as reference points to anchor their conversations with customers. The product in ques-tion would typically include a range of styles and price points so that the products could easily be called upon at an opportune time. A word to the wise, though: Be careful when selecting products for your reference points. They shouldn't be too narrow in style, price, or aesthetic orienta-tion. If your own taste is too specific, it may not align with a broad enough base of customers to align with a good positioning strategy.

Select a range of styles and price points, and familiarize yourself with as many details as you need on those specific pieces to be able to com-petently and confidently talk about them. Although you may actually sell some of these pieces from time to time, the more important learning being provided here is that the selected products will become valuable tools in your discovery process with your customers. They become, in the best-case scenario, a part of your narrative to uncover customer needs.

Do not overwhelm your customer with infinite and irrelevant prod-uct details, and do not use your preselected items to product-dump, an unusually irksome and wholly ineffective way to engage customers. Utilize your favorite products to authentically demonstrate your passion and pride in your company and work. Use them as a genuine way to communicate the quality and value of your products and the customer experience. Use the products as a way to show that you too are a customer, and you yourself would sincerely love to own the products in question. That kind of connection is very powerful as you communicate as much through your body language as you do in what you say.

Leonard Mlodinow wrote in *Subliminal: How Your Unconscious Mind Rules Your Behavior*: "Language is handy, but we humans have social and emotional connections that transcend words, and are communicated—and understood—without conscious thought." That kind of emotive transference is more powerful than any product details you might have memorized and regurgitated. Instead, this says, "I believe in this product, I would want to own this myself."

Product information is not a weapon to be sharpened every day so that unsuspecting customers can be slain at will by your great intellect and boundless knowledge. Take the time to understand what your store's products and services are. Embrace every opportunity to fully explore the different product categories, and try to uncover interesting details and nuances that you can deploy as appropriate. Understand the important features and take the time to note how those features might benefit your customers.

Charleen Plaff, who has a distinguished career managing retail stores, shared the following story about an experience that became pivotal in her career:

> I was hired to manage a store that was underperforming and had, for various reasons, only two employees left when I got there, an office manager and a part-time salesperson. It was already mid-October, and I had to hire and train an entire staff before the holiday season.
>
> To make a long story short, I hired six employees, all young and without any jewelry knowledge, in a very short period of time. Not surprisingly, the other managers in the company thought that I was crazy. I had to move so fast that I had no time to contemplate the consequences of building a team of inexperienced

salespeople so close to the season. There was quite simply no time for a plan B.

Despite my belief in each of the new hires, I had my doubts about how I was going to get them all trained in time to make the Christmas business happen. We undertook a program of intense daily training, just to give the team the very basics. The daily repetition seemed to be showing results, but the salespeople occasionally wore a look of mild panic on their faces, and they were forgiven for questioning their abilities to be successful in such a short period of time. Beneath my calm exterior, I too was scared as all heck.

What I was confident about, however, was that I had hired each and every one of them for their ability to connect with people, and because of their natural energy and enthusiasm. I decided to allay their fears a little by removing as much of the "technical" portion of their training as was possible. I was afraid that too much technical information would trip them up and make them less certain in their customer interactions .(We've all seen the "data-dump" sales presentations, and I knew that wouldn't work.)

I told the team to forget about selling diamonds and jewelry, but to think more in terms of "symbols of love." They learned to introduce themselves and then to emotionally connect with their clients before ever opening a case. They would ask the customer who the gift was for and what message the client wanted to give with the gift. I had each of them pick out their favorite piece in each category and learn everything about those particular items. They used those pieces of jewelry as go-to items to show their clients and tell a story. If the sales associate loved the items, and could confidently speak to their attributes, they would look and sound professional, and that confidence would readily translate to the clients.

To our delight, the strategy worked! The pressure was gone, we had smiling faces everywhere—on salespeople and on our customers—and we were all engaged and energized in a way that I had not seen in the business up to that point. The atmosphere in the store was happy and festive, and we became a cohesive team that genuinely liked each other as we executed our clear plan of action.

I encouraged the sales team to help each other in their presentations, offering their "favorite" items whenever the opportunity presented itself. Team-selling became the norm, everyone shared their strengths . . . we had a blast! Customers enjoyed not being "sold to," and they told us we weren't like the other stores.

In a store that had never exceed $1.1 million in annual sales, our "little engine that could" sales team exceeded $500,000 in December alone, more than double what might reasonably have been expected.

What I learned as a manager and as a sales professional in those two short months is that clients don't want to be sold to. They could have gone to any jewelry store and gotten bombarded with product information. They could have found any number of "qualified salespeople" in our competitors' stores and still not bought anything. What they wanted, and what they found in our store, was a team of people who had great pride in what they were doing. We all believed in our mission to have fun, to listen to our customers, to emotionally connect with them and with each other. They dedicated themselves to learning all that they could in the small windows of opportunity after they were hired, but they never allowed that product knowledge, or lack thereof, to distract them from their mission of satisfying their customers.

As a side note, two of those young people went on to become very successful managers in our company, and another one of them became a top diamond salesperson in his very first year.

Charleen took lemons and made lemonade. She didn't have the luxury of constructing a seasoned team of industry veterans over an extended period of time, and so she was, by necessity, forced to underscore her own philosophy about sales being so much more than tenure and product knowledge, by hiring people without experience. She built her team based on traits that are untrainable: attitude, energy, and positivity. She provided the basic product orientation so that each of her team members had some measure of confidence to go along with their can-do attitude, and it worked. In fact, as her numbers indicated, it paid out in spades. Charleen did not attempt to drown her new team in product information that they realistically could never have absorbed in such a short period of time, instead, she encouraged them to utilize their inherent talents and infuse that wiring with just enough product knowledge to be credible and confident.

Jonah Berger wrote in *Contagious: Why Things Catch On*, "People don't think in terms of information. They think in terms of narratives. But while people focus on the story itself, information comes along for the ride." Having product knowledge is a good thing. Being able to use it wisely is a very good thing. Assuming that having lots of it necessarily makes for a good salesperson . . . well, that's just a thing—no salesperson should bet their future on that.

Building Value

"The emotional tail wags the rational dog."

—JONATHAN HAIDT

The first real job I had in the United States was at a jewelry store called Lebolt & Company on State Street in Chicago. I didn't know it when I started, but the store had become part of the Whitehall Jewelers group of stores, and it came with some of the most creative pricing strategies in the industry. I can still remember the codes on the price tags that told the salesperson (purportedly) what the actual cost of the item was. The letters on the price tag could be interpreted by us "astute" salespeople, and we would then have a guideline as to how much we could discount a piece. Theoretically, the greater the disparity between the cost and the printed "retail" price, the deeper the discount we could offer.

When I first started working at Lebolt's, I spent a lot of noncustomer time acquainting myself with the products and, in particular, reading the tickets to better understand the cost/retail relationship. Without the slightest exaggeration, I can tell you that the experience was a culture shock to me. In some instances, I was seeing costs that were ten to fifteen percent of the retail price. Of course, the "retail price" was nothing more than a launching pad for a silly conversation about what we would actually be willing to sell the item for, especially if they bought the item *today*. The idea that we wouldn't do that same "deal" the next day was as laughable as the ticket prices themselves, but I digress.

I had never experienced anything like that working in jewelry shops in Ireland, and it was disorienting and disconcerting. To survive, I tried to engage the customers, absent the pretense of either one of us believing that the ticket price had any merit, but with an implicit understanding that if we worked together, we could make a deal that both of us could live with.

Without a doubt, that particular business model not only defied logic, it was, in my view, immoral and deceptive. It presupposed that there was a basis of truth (and there wasn't) in the ticket prices and that the consumer ought to place some measure of trust in the company (and they shouldn't have). Whitehall Jewelers went out of business a few years ago, and despite knowing many good people who went through that organization, that a business model inherently based on price deception should have survived even as long as it did still surprises me.

If you believe that every customer who walks in your door wants the cheapest price, then you will be proven right. You will bring that implicit bias into your every interaction, and you will, by default, expect the very least of your customers. In short, believing that every customer is driven to get the lowest price is really your way of saying that you possess neither the will nor the capacity to influence and inspire your customer to a higher aspiration.

I did not, as they say, come from money. My father was a house painter, and we had to make do with what he was able to provide for our family. We didn't buy luxury products, and, quite frankly, we wouldn't have recognized luxury if we were paid to do so. Of course, we knew the difference between a nice house in a nice neighborhood and our working-class house and our working-class neighborhood. We could appreciate what a great car looked like, as opposed to the old beat-up Volkswagen Beetle (the original Beetle) and Ford Anglia my dad drove. But we didn't really *do* luxury. We didn't know what designer clothes, bags, vacations, or jewelry looked like. When we had vacations, or holidays, as we'd call them, it entailed piling our lot into the small car and driving across the country to Galway, where we'd scale the walls of orchards and steal apples for fun. We would occasionally fly the short distance to London and stay with my grandparents in their small council house in Middlesex.

It wasn't until I started working for Tiffany & Co. in 1986 that I began to understand the transformative powers of a great product and a great experience. Even in that earlier iteration of Tiffany, it was clear that our customers felt special when they entered the hallowed halls of the Chicago store, and there was a certain dignity and decorum that was, more often than not, present in our interactions. A couple of notable exceptions include the customer who complained about my "obdurate demeanor," as we ultimately stopped his endless cycle of buy-and-return on the same item. It was not so much a buying experience for him as it was his sport of choice, tormenting us, that is. The second example was the friend of a former employee who continually tried to return, for a refund, all of the tabletop and gift products our former employee had stolen from us over the few years of her employment. As we might say in Dublin, "the bloody cheek of that one!"

To put my newfound appreciation for value versus price into perspective, I was living in the western suburbs of Chicago. There was a shopping strip close to my house, and we would occasionally visit the Service Merchandise store to buy small household items and gifts. For those of you who are too young to remember Service Merchandise, it was a catalog showroom, all very clean and organized and, to be honest, quite sterile and devoid of any real ambience or warmth. Nonetheless, it was often a default trip when we needed a gift that wouldn't break the bank.

Service Merchandise, like Spiegel and Sears, had served the market very well for years. If you had a baby shower or a wedding to attend, you were sure to find something—a lamp, a toaster. Whatever your budget, Service Merchandise would serve you well. Except, it didn't. There was, of course, the appearance of value—you got what you paid for—and it was functional and reasonably easy to navigate.

What Service Merchandise lacked was the transformative power that great retail experiences provide. You just never came away from a visit to that store with the same sense of pure joy that a trip to Tiffany's would provide. There was nothing uplifting or experiential about the visit. It didn't tap into your aspiration or sense of wonder. You didn't visit with a heightened sense of anticipation or leave giddy with delight at what your gift would say to the recipient.

Great retail experiences are transformative and, to borrow a term from MasterCard, priceless. There are lots of people who prefer to shop in stores that advertise cheaper prices, and there will always be a demand for cheap prices, be that at outlet malls, Kmart, Ocean State Job Lot, or even Walmart. In my own business, there are infinite numbers of retail jewelry stores that operate under the premise that he who discounts the most wins. Good luck with that! Unless you are big enough to operate on Costco-type margins and you are in a no-service, low-overhead business, chasing the customer's dollar to the bottom is not a good strategy.

For any salesperson to presume to know a customers' desires, to make the decision that they will only buy at discount, to present them with lesser-quality goods is, quite frankly, sacrilegious to the industry. There are entirely too many salespeople and too many businesses that appeal to the lowest common denominator and, in doing so, do no favors whatsoever to either the customer or the business.

Have you ever wondered why certain salespeople seem to have no issues closing larger sales while others almost never write big tickets? The latter group might otherwise be quite effective, nurturing their customers and producing an acceptable level of sales performance, but they just can't seem to get over the hump when it comes to larger tickets.

When I started to notice this phenomenon many years ago, I assumed that it was tied into the salesperson's background. If he or she had grown up in an environment surrounded by material goods, I reasoned that they would have a greater comfort level selling more expensive jewelry, as opposed to people like myself who were products of a less-privileged upbringing. However, I soon found out that that wasn't the case. While some of the best salespeople did come from more privileged backgrounds, others did not.

Perhaps it was a matter of tenure, I thought. I began to look for a correlation between tenure and high-ticket performance, but once again I found that there was none. Some of the people with whom I had worked had been in retail jewelry for many years, while others were new to the business and could still perform at a high level.

The next area I considered was industry education. Surely, I thought, those salespeople with a better levels of education across the various industry institutions, and with the higher-end brands, would have more confidence and greater success in making higher-ticket sales? Alas, they did not. In fact, I found an inverse relationship between what I'll call "industry pedigree" and sales acumen. It was as if those people who were most drawn to professional certification and continuing education had the least amount of talent for sales. So what is it? Why do some excel at higher-end and luxury sales while others do not?

It boils down to value judgments and biases. If the salesperson believes that a given product is too expensive, they will be one hundred percent correct in determining that the customer cannot afford it. Short of opening the case and selecting the merchandise for themselves, customers who are being waited on by salespeople who bring their own value judgments and biases into the interaction will have a much more difficult time selecting higher-end (a relative term, I fully accept) merchandise.

My wife once shared with me how a salesperson exclaimed, about her own company's product, that she couldn't imagine why anyone would pay that much. Well, in her case, she was correct. People didn't buy those products from her because, just when the circumstances were right, she ruined the mood by revealing that even she, the employee, thought the prices were too expensive.

Value perception is more about architecture than archeology. The salesperson's job is to build value by painting a picture and aligning the proposed solution to the customer's needs. It is not about deciphering every conceivable attribute and feature of a given product. It is not about beating the customer into submission with facts and figures until they relent. Marc Lewis wrote in *The Biology of Desire*, "Choice is biological too. And choice, while it may look rational upon quick inspection, is driven more by motivation than by abstract reasoning."

As obvious as it may seem, one of the best ways to overcome biases and value judgments is to have the conversation with your salespeople about why they should never decide what the customer can and cannot afford. Their job is to ask good open-ended questions. Questions such as "Tell me what you are looking to accomplish today" and "Tell me about your wife. What kinds of things have you bought for her in the past?" can be very revealing and nonthreatening.

Once the salesperson has asked the appropriate questions, listened intently to the answers, and observed the customer's body language, it is okay to ask, "What price range did you have in mind?" That question must be earned, however, as it should not be asked until a meaningful connection has been made with the customer and a profile of his or her needs has emerged.

After the price range has been established, the salesperson should present three options to the customer that align with what he or she has been able to uncover in their conversation with them. The first option should be generally at the price level (baseline) indicated by the customer. The second option should be a reasonable step up (fifty percent higher), and the third option can be one hundred percent greater than the baseline price.

The customer's baseline price serves as a primer that makes the other prices relevant, and by having that baseline price in play, the pressure is off the customer. He or she can relax and focus on the value proposition the salesperson has built with each of the three options. I'll get into the three options and the different price points in the chapters on paradox of choice and the contrast principle.

When a customer is reluctant to volunteer a price range, a very safe way to approach that challenge is to pull out one of the most expensive items you have in the store (know it beforehand) and to present that to the customer. You'll usually get a nervous laugh. The customer will let their guard down and usually volunteer a price. Every once in a while, though, you'll be the one who is shocked when your seemingly unattainable option gains traction.

As difficult as it is to offload our own biases and to refrain from making value judgments, a great deal of progress can be made simply by recognizing that we have them. That, and a simple process of using the customer's price range as the anchor of a three-step product offering, can help salespeople deliver bigger sales and better experiences.

It is not your job to decide for the customer; you must inspire and influence the direction of the interaction by questioning and listening, and by recognizing that it is never your job to decide what the customer will or will not spend. Recognize that value and price are not the same thing. Price is what someone pays for something, and value is what a product does for them now and in the days, weeks, and months to come. The appreciation for value will last long past the point where the customer has forgotten what he or she paid for the product.

Priming

The principle of priming is ubiquitous in our lives. Obvious examples can be found in subtle and not-so-subtle product placements in television shows and movies. If you watch the movie *Jurassic World*, you will notice that a subplot to the marauding dinosaurs seems to be that the whole island has been taken over by Mercedes-Benz vehicles. Every time an SUV pulls up, the camera strategically frames the shot to show the iconic Mercedes-Benz logo. Likewise, if you have ever watched an episode of *American Idol*, you probably couldn't help but notice the ever-present Coca Cola cups sitting in front of the panelists, with the logos in full view of the millions watching.

Beyond traditional marketing, or, more appropriately, sitting just beneath the surface of traditional marketing, we are constantly exposed to signals and inferences designed to influence our behavior, and understanding that subtle and not-so-subtle psychology can be a very effective tool in a sales environment. For instance, if we go into a coffee shop and we notice a strategically positioned tip jar, we are more likely to tip than if there is no jar. For service people, musicians, and just about anyone else who would like to solicit tips, the single most effective thing they can do is to put a few dollar bills into the jar and, in doing so, prime the customers and listeners into making further contributions.

William Poundstone wrote in *Priceless*, "Priming affects not only what you notice but what you do." Good examples in retail might include the practice in department stores of putting complete outfits onto manne-quins. You can, of course, go to the appropriate area to see a selection of suits or ties, shirts or shoes, but when you see the entire outfit pulled together on that mannequin, you are more likely to buy additional items beyond just the product that you originally intended to purchase. The mannequin has effectively created a context for you to view what might be possible and, oftentimes without realizing it, you have been repro-grammed to expand your horizons and your budget.

We respond to cues and signals, oftentimes unconsciously, and one can make a case that priming might actually be more effective than tra-ditional up-selling or cross-selling in influencing a customer's behavior. Priming serves to shape customers' perceptions in a very nonthreatening way, as it is less obviously self-serving than a salesperson overtly trying to get you to buy more stuff.

One of the very best examples of priming I have ever heard of came from Ricky Wubnig. He told me that his store had brought in a new line of inexpensive bracelets. They were made to be stacked and, at thirty-two dollars apiece, a woman could wear multiple bracelets at the same time and create her own unique look.

After bringing the line in, Ricky watched his salespeople for a couple of weeks to gather needed intelligence, and he noticed a recurring pat-tern: customers would ask salespeople how much the bracelets cost and, unsurprisingly, the salespeople would respond by answering the ques-tion very directly. As Ricky analyzed the sales of the bracelets, he discov-ered that customers were buying a single bracelet about 25 percent of the time and two bracelets about 75 percent of the time. His inclination was that bracelet sales ought to be much higher, and that each customer should be buying more of them on each transaction.

Having given a great deal of thought to the dilemma, he quite bril-liantly implemented a remarkable example of priming by changing the language his salespeople used each time a customer asked how much the bracelets cost. He instructed the team to say, "The bracelets are thirty-two dollars each, and customers generally buy five or six of them."

That specific language was a brilliant invention on his part and it had an enormous effect on sales. Given that the store ultimately ended up selling about $3 million annually of those bracelets, it would be no exaggeration to suggest that the salespeople's adjusted response likely contributed an additional $1.5–$2 million dollars in annual sales.

Ricky's directive to the team was priming at its magical best. The salespeople were setting the table for their customers by subtly creating a way for them to think about the bracelets. The store's customers had been buying one or two, and they would never have given a moment's thought to the notion that there was anything unusual in that. Once the salespeople changed their language to unconsciously paint a picture for the customer, they readily stepped into that space and were very happy to conform to the new expectation that had been set for them. The customers never knew that people before them had been buying one or two of the bracelets, and so they readily stepped into the context for buying that Ricky's team had established with their new language. They were more than happy to buy five or six at a time.

Other examples of priming relate to mood and body language. Have you ever noticed how your mood tends to change to reflect the mood of the people around you? The next time you are in line,—checking into a hotel, boarding a plane, waiting to pay for something in the pharmacy— just watch how people infect and reflect the environment around them. If the person scanning tickets at the jet bridge happens to do so with a smile and a kind word to the boarding passengers, watch how that attitude influences how the passengers respond to them. Conversely, if the gate agent does not smile, make eye contact, or have anything to say to the passengers, that attitude also tends to be reflected back by the boarding passengers.

In a recent flight from Rochester to Newark, the lone flight attendant on my entirely too small plane went through his preflight announcements and then finished his inspiring speech with the following piece of dog doo-doo: "If our flight is smooth, I will be providing coffee and water service." It was a six a.m. flight, and we passengers were already borderline comatose from our respective early starts and the shockingly small space into which so many of us were squeezed.

The flight attendant had a quiet and attentive audience—if you don't count the sleepers—and his announcing job should have been routine and uneventful. His ill-advised reminder that we *might* encounter unfriendly skies was neither warranted nor welcomed. After he had finished speaking, nobody said anything, except for a woman a couple of rows behind me who said, "Ugh, that's encouraging."

Quite unnecessarily, the flight attendant had negatively primed us for the possibility of a bad experience. Thankfully, the flight was as comfortable as it could be under the ridiculous conditions that air travelers are usually subjected to nowadays, however, our guardian of the skies had introduced a negative tone at the very outset with his ill-advised announcement, and it had a deflating effect on those of us who were not sleeping.

We set the tone for how we want events to unfold by how we communicate in words, attitude, and demeanor. The aroma of coffee and a green wall may trigger a desire to visit a Starbucks. The smell of popcorn and a red wall may elicit a craving for a Coke, popcorn, and a movie. A welcome smile and eye contact will communicate warmth and engagement, and the smell of cooked food, when you enter your local Wegmans or Whole Foods, will generally result in your buying a whole lot more food than you otherwise anticipated. Or, as I experienced, when the flight attendant on a Wright brothers–sized plane tells you that he will serve coffee and water *if* we don't encounter turbulence . . . well, you get the picture.

A very obvious but not particularly well-practiced example of positive priming happens when you first engage a customer in your store. After you have welcomed them and asked a probing question or two, you should always tell them (via priming) that you will ensure they have a good experience and that you will help them make the best choice for them. Be clear and sincere about that sentiment, as it sends a positive message to the customer and it sets you, psychologically, along the path to understanding that your role is to satisfy their needs and to actually make the sale, not provide a bunch of information and *maybe* make the sale and *maybe* take care of the customer's needs.

Priming sets the tone; it provides an important context, and it offers a wonderful opportunity to frame a conversation and a connection that can be a win-win for both the salesperson and the customer. The simple statement "we're going to make sure that we get you taken care of today" can go a long way toward relaxing a customer and convincing them that they can trust you to attend to their needs, as opposed to you just driving your own agenda or, Heaven help us, filling space.

The Customer Experience

"We are not in the coffee business serving people, we
are in the people business serving coffee."

—HOWARD SCHULTZ

I took my kids to the mall some time ago to have lunch and to run a couple of errands. We had to pick up a phone charger at the Apple store for my son, Killian, and I needed a new pillow for my bed.

When we walked into the Apple store, we were struck, as usual, by the well-lit, energy-filled environment. The store was well-staffed with logo-attired and readily accessible Apple specialists. My son walked to the back of the store and grabbed himself a charger, and, after the specialist pointed out the fact that my son had inadvertently selected the wrong cord, he himself hurried off to retrieve the right one. He then quickly swiped my credit card on his handheld device, and we were on our way. We were in and out of the store in about ninety seconds, and the experience couldn't have been any easier.

Our next port of call was Sears. When we entered, our purposeful striding soon descended into a slow, challenging scouting mission, as we sought out the department that might contain pillows and/or someone wearing appropriately branded attire to direct us there. Long before we found the latter, we eventually stumbled on the pillows, and I was able to find my new bedfellow.

Our adventure recommenced. We now had to find somewhere to pay for it. We walked and walked, finding only unstaffed registers. Eventually, we found a place to pay for the pillow and joined the long line of customers who had eventually, like us, found the Promised Land, the place where we could finally pay for our purchases and escape to Johnny Rockets and lunch.

We took our place behind the other previously lost souls, and I couldn't help but notice the different emotions between the customers and employees, as compared to our Apple experience. Our building agitation was palpable, and it was in complete contrast to the indifference of the two Sears employees behind the counter, who conducted themselves as though there was no waiting line of customers at all. They displayed no urgency or energy, and any modicum of civility was lost in their complete lack of engagement with us or, for that matter, with each other.

After an interminable wait, I ascended to number two in line, and it was there that I overheard one of the employees demanding of the customer in front of me, "Why are you returning this?" The question itself was not unreasonable; the employee must surely have to account for the specific reason for the return in their point-of-sale system. The customer may have changed her mind, or the product might have been defective. The tone, however, is what I noticed. It was accusatory and clearly agitated, befitting a courtroom prosecutor and delivered as if the customer had committed some egregious crime.

We finally paid for the pillow and walked off together to get lunch, and the kids and I talked about our shopping experiences at the two stores. As teenagers, they had no inkling of Sears' storied history as one of the great merchants and retailers. They hadn't heard of the Sears catalogue and they wouldn't understand how previous generations had almost defaulted to Sears for linens, for clothes, for televisions and phones, for washing machines, and even for tires. All they knew was that Apple got them in and out quickly and efficiently and, well . . . Sears didn't.

Our experience echoed what Dixon, Toman, and DeLisi wrote in *The Effortless Experience*:

> We love the Apple Store—but not for the reasons you might think. Sure, it's open and airy, sleek and cool, filled with enough technological wizardry to occupy even the most shopping-averse person for hours. But we'd argue that one of the keys to the Apple Store's success—why they've been able to bring in more revenue per square foot than any other retailer on earth—is because Apple has focused ruthlessly on making its in-store experience a *low-effort* experience.

Our Apple experience could not have been any more "low-effort," and our Sears experience was a stark reminder of the vast chasm that exists between retailers who "get it" and retailers who don't.

One retailer who totally gets it is Blake from Florida. A colleague and I were visiting with him some time ago, and we ended up spending a little more time than we had anticipated in his store. There were lots of customers coming in and out, and the interactions provided a wonderful glimpse into how sales and service ought to be delivered. I was fascinated watching Blake, the store's primary salesperson and partial owner of the business, perform his magic. His manner with his customers was warm, welcoming, and authentic. He greeted everyone as though each was a welcome guest in his home, and he gave them all of his attention and positive energy. I am not a fan of retailers using the term "guest" to describe their customers. I find it to be a tad naive, if not downright pretentious. Watching Blake, however, was probably the closest I have ever come to believing the term to be warranted.

As I observed his body language, it was clear to me, as it was to each of his customers, that there was no place else he would rather be at that moment, no one else he would rather be with, and nothing else he would rather do than to spend time with each of those customers. His total commitment to each person he worked with was broken only once, when he excused himself to grab a bottle of cold water for the UPS delivery man. It was about ninety-five degrees outside, and I have no doubt that Blake's consideration was appreciated by the UPS guy, and duly noted by the customer he momentarily left, who seemed pleased to be interrupted for his kind act.

There was one couple in particular who Blake seemed to really connect with, and I watched as he made a fourteen-thousand-dollar sale. The whole mood was one of great celebration, and what struck me with this particular interaction was that it was very evident Blake expected nothing less than to make the sale. His friendly, easy, and authentic manner with the couple masked a steely resolve to actually make the business happen. He clearly saw no contradiction between providing great service to his clients and asking them for money. He expects to close sales, and he is frequently rewarded for that expectation. To paraphrase the great football coach Vince Lombardi, when Blake made the sale, he acted like he'd been in the end zone before.

After the big sale, as this particular couple thanked Blake and began to leave the store, he called them back and said he would like them to have something. With that, he reached into a drawer and pulled out a beautiful bathrobe, presenting it to the woman and telling her that his mom had ordered them and that they came from the same place that makes the bathrobes for the Ritz-Carlton.

The sale had already been made and the customers had no knowledge that there was a gift with purchase. The store had not advertised that giveaway, and there was no sense of it being quid pro quo. It was simply an exclamation point on a wonderful experience for everyone. I imagined the sheer delight for the customers as they retold that story to their friends in the days and weeks following. What do you think the likelihood of them revisiting that store is?

Contrast Blake's story with the experience of the writer Philip Delves Broughton. In his book *The Art of the Sale*, he wrote about his own experience in buying an engagement ring:

I went into the process in a rather typical state of bachelor panic, fearful of both the expense and the risk of buying something that would undermine all the hard work I had already put into convincing my girlfriend that I was worthy of being promoted to spouse. The first store I visited was Van Cleef & Arpels on the ground floor of the Bergdorf Goodman building on Fifth Avenue. I felt uncomfortable the moment I entered. There were no visible prices, just glass cases full of glittering gems and predatory-looking salespeople. I felt like a mark, the kind they must have seen a thousand times: single dumb male in search of a ring. My next stop was Forty-Seventh Street, New York's diamond district, a jewelry bazaar. The problem here was not lack of choice, but overabundance. Every store had everything at every price, to the point where I ceased to trust anything.

Broughton's experience, unfortunately, is not unusual. As he said, he had done the hard part by convincing his girlfriend that he was "worthy of being promoted to spouse," and yet he had to endure a harrowing experience on both ends of the spectrum, from the deal-makers on Forty-Seventh Street to the "predatory-looking" salespeople in some of the higher-end stores. It is a pity that Broughton did not find himself in Blake's store, where he would surely have enjoyed an entirely different experience and would likely have felt very different about what was surely one of the most important purchases of his life.

I stayed at the aforementioned Ritz-Carlton in Chicago a while back. I was working at a trade show, and when I returned to my room at the end of the day, I noticed that housekeeping had left a bookmark on the front of a book I was reading and had left sitting on the desk. The bookmark said, "Reading is like dreaming with your eyes open." It is a quote by the graphic novelist YoYo. I would assume that the Ritz-Carlton buys those bookmarks in large quantities and delivers them to their various properties around the world. The cost of a single one is clearly less than the price of a bar of soap they change every single day in their bathrooms, even after minimal use. The impact, however, was absolutely priceless for this particular guest and voracious reader. To have trained their housekeeping team to the extent that they would recognize an opportunity to make such a lovely gesture as putting that bookmark on top of my book really says something about them. It impressed me to no end, and I not only continue to enjoy using it (currently residing in *Joseph Anton*, Salman Rushdie's memoir), I readily share the story any chance I get. A small but powerful touch that cost virtually nothing but brought a smile to my face and gave me a memorable little vignette to recall and retell.

As I write this section, I am flying on a JetBlue plane from San Juan to Boston. It is a Friday night, and I have had a crazy week. I am struck, not for the first time, at how JetBlue seems to have lost the opportunity to establish a superlative customer experience at a time when our expectations as flyers have never been lower. The new and clean planes, the exciting logo, the friendly staff, and the free bags have given way to a sameness and, for me at least, a sense of the rote and routine. The staff no longer appear to be any friendlier than any of the other airlines, they now charge for checked bags, and just about everything seems to have been repositioned as a potential revenue stream rather than an opportunity to make their customers more comfortable.

This flight is a classic example. The "even more legroom" section seems to be expanding, and numerous seats, indeed rows, sit open and unoccupied while weary travelers are crushed into the remaining seats. Given that the flight is almost four hours long, and I have had a particularly hectic few days of travel, I took the airline up on their offer to move me to an exit row for an additional fifty dollars. When I moved up, I found myself alone in a row of three exit-row seats. I also noticed that the exit row across from me was completely unoccupied, as were most of the even-more-legroom seats ahead of me.

Besides the obvious question I have—how safe it is to have exit rows sitting completely empty—why has JetBlue concluded that opportunities to move some folks around in situations like this, creating space and a good deal more comfort for many more passengers, is not good service?

We can, of course, imagine the conversation at JetBlue's headquarters when the question of customer comfort comes up: "You know, if we start moving people around when we have empty seats, we'll never sell the upgrades."

I wonder if the current attitude at JetBlue reflects the values the company espoused at the outset. I suspect not. An opportunity missed for sure, and another example of a company descending into that dreaded middle space—neither the cheapest price nor the best service.

As important as it is to articulate what the customer experience must be in retail stores, it all falls apart if we don't deliver on whatever that promise is. Apple lives their promise each and every day, Sears does not—and is paying the price for it, and JetBlue seems to have lost sight of the great opportunity they had to really distinguish themselves in a space that is riddled with indifference and apathy.

Customer service is what we do, not what we say, and it must be about delivering a service, a product, and an experience that is in the *customer's* best interest, not yours. As Apple so wonderfully demonstrated, get me in and get me out. If I want to hang around your store, I will do so on my schedule, not yours. I don't want to work hard to find whatever it was I came in for; I expect that to be handled by engaged, caring and, most of all, efficient salespeople. I expect to be asked for the sale. In fact, I would be disappointed if I was not. I do not, however, want to be hostage to the store's disorganization and dysfunction, or some misguided sense that keeping me around for longer than suits my schedule makes for a good customer experience.

Earning Your Customers' Trust

"It is discouraging how many people are shocked by honesty and how few by deceit."

—NOEL COWARD

Retailer Tammy Geraci told me about a sale that both invigorated her passion and love for what she does and underscored the way she and her team have created lasting moments and built great trust over the years. It is the kind of story that happens on a regular basis in Tammy's store, and yet we are all too often in danger of not appreciating or understanding how very impactful stories like this are to those people involved or, quite frankly, the hard work and commitment that goes into making them a reality. As Tammy told it:

Mike's mom, Mary, stopped in to see us one day. She lives in Avon Lake, and she has been a great customer for many years. I could tell, however, that there was something a little different about this particular visit. She seemed to have an added spring in her step, and I realized why when she told me what had brought her in. Her son, Mike, who had accompanied her on many of her visits through the years, had joined the US military (thank you very much!), and he had met and fallen in love with a young woman on base. He wanted to ask her to marry him, and he had asked his mom to visit with us to see if we could help him with a ring.

I was, needless to say, delighted for Mike, and though it had seemed like just yesterday that he had been running around our store as a little kid, here he was now serving our country and about to get married—and we were being asked to help with his ring. Mike asked his mom to talk to us because he was stationed overseas in Afghanistan. I've never been in the military, but this felt like a mission to me, and I couldn't have been more proud to have been entrusted with such an important task as helping to shape his special moment.

Shortly after Mary's visit, Mike contacted me from Afghanistan, and I was thrilled to work with him in the ensuing weeks to create a beautiful ring for his bride-to-be. When the ring was ready, we sent it to him overseas and waited, with fingers crossed, and with an occasional skipped heartbeat, to make sure he loved it and, more importantly, that his intended loved it.

After what seemed like an interminable wait—but which was really just a few weeks—an email arrived from Mike with the news that everything had gone fantastically well. He and his girlfriend went for an unforgettable trip to New Zealand, where, atop the beautiful setting of one of the country's many breathtaking glaciers, Mike popped the question and she said yes. The photos that he sent to us were just wonderful, and we couldn't have been any more excited for the happy couple.

These moments make it all worthwhile for me and for our team. It doesn't feel like work when we get the opportunity to help write our customers' stories. It is all the more rewarding when we have the privilege of serving them from one generation to the next. That Mike trusted us to do this, while he was six thousand miles away serving our country, was a great privilege for us.

There are certain things that are so obvious as to be redundant. We don't have to be told to get dressed in the morning, to brush our teeth, or to eat when we are hungry. We don't need reminding to dress warm in winter or to stop at red lights when we are driving. Yet, somehow, it still seems appropriate to remind the reader that salespeople must always be honest with their customers. Without personal integrity, no salesperson can build the foundation of a credible career, and without building trust, stories like Tammy's would be far too rare.

It would be great if there was no need to remind salespeople that they ought to be honest and transparent with their customers, but there are entirely too many customers who believe that salespeople would readily lie to them to make a sale, and unfortunately, there is some truth in that stereotype.

Certain sales professions seem to be more tainted than others. Used-car salesmen and insurance salesmen come readily to mind as people who have to overcome that perception. Anyone who has ever sold time-shares has had to fight an uphill battle, and unfortunately there are salespeople of questionable character trying to make a living in retail by using any means necessary to make the sale.

The downside of not being honest with your customer is obvious enough. You can miss sales, lose a customer completely, or invite returns of sales that were force-fed and cast doubt on you and on the integrity of your store. Once compromised, it is almost impossible to win back the trust of a scorned customer. I cannot think of any sale that could be important enough to justify jeopardizing a long-term relationship with a customer, and yet there are too many people employed in sales who regularly take such risks.

My experience with successful salespeople shows that they prize honesty with their customers and colleagues. In fact, their transparency with their coworkers sometimes comes at a price and can make them very unpopular, probably something to do with "not suffering fools."

While being honest with your clients can occasionally lead to your customer walking out of the store empty-handed, the longer-term benefits of being truthful far outweigh the narrow and selfish interest served by misleading your customer.

A former colleague and friend, John McBarron, shared one such story. He told me that a man walked into his store one morning wearing a rather consternated look on his face and holding a Tiffany box in his hand. The box contained a Tiffany private-label watch that he wished to return. He had purchased the timepiece over the phone from a personal shopper, and he felt like she really hadn't listened to him. He had quite specifically requested an alligator watch-strap on his timepiece and been assured by the personal shopper that his request would be handled accordingly, and yet, somehow, the watch had arrived with a lizard strap.

It was certainly possible that the personal shopper hadn't known the difference between lizard and alligator. It is also possible that the entry-level price point watch the customer wanted created budget issues that would not allow for the added expense of the alligator strap. In any case, the customer didn't get what he asked for, and John was faced with the prospect of having to somehow make good.

"I wear alligator, not lizard. Look at my belt, look at my shoes," said the agitated customer. He then lifted his leg to show the evidence. "You should see my luggage, it is magnificent."

John described the customer as being well dressed and, despite his obvious disappointment, not entirely unpleasant.

"May I be frank with you?" John asked. "I'm looking at the way you are dressed and I agree with you, I just don't see you in this watch. I see you in something much more elegant."

The simple and honest observation from John had captured the customer's interest, and he replied, surprised and intrigued by the John's directness, "What do you see me in?"

John pointed out another watch that had an alligator strap, and which seemed to him to be a much better fit, and suggested that one instead.

The watch was five times more expensive than the piece the customer was returning.

The customer tried on the watch and then asked, "So, you would take this one back and sell me that one instead?"

"That's right," John replied.

"I love it," the customer replied, and he told John that he had just made his day.

The customer had come in with a problem and, thanks to an astute observation from the salesperson, and respectfully direct and honest feedback, a more significant sale was made and, more importantly, the seeds of a relationship were sown. In turn, the customer had appreciated John's honesty and was happy to reward him and the store with a considerably larger sale and, we can assume, the likelihood of continued patronage.

John told me that he was ecstatic for two days. He had initially worried that he might have crossed the line by being too direct with the customer, and yet they had both been rewarded because of his integrity. As John recounted, "I had made many larger sales before and since, but having the customer tell me that I had made his day was a great feeling. I was being very honest with him, and he respected that."

John and Tammy's stories are two ends of the same narrative—building trust. Tammy was rewarded for having built her relationship over two generations, and John had an opportunity to begin that journey with his customer. Understanding that every customer interaction, both new and repeat, provides an opportunity to deliver and reinforce that trust is central to the process of relationship building. It doesn't mean that you will always make a sale or that you will always have the answer to the customer's needs on a given day, but you will have earned the right to be in that conversation again and again, and those opportunities are the foundation upon which we build great retail businesses.

Paradox of Choice

"I truly don't have any formula for the choices I make."

—JAVIER BARDEM

Have you ever visited a Cheesecake Factory restaurant? If you have not, let me set the table for you. The food is, on the whole, pretty decent; the ambiance, for a larger restaurant, is warm and inviting; and the prices are not overly expensive. Here's the bad news: Cheesecake Factory does not so much provide a menu as they give you a veritable tome to navigate. The mega-menu is filled with so many options that diners could become paralyzed from a multitude of options and the fear of making the wrong decision.

As I turn each page of the huge menu, my world becomes a blur, but since I was persuaded by someone to make a reservation or had to wait for an hour to be seated, eventually I settle on some dish or other, not entirely convinced that I've selected the right meal. Second-guessing becomes the order of the day, as I question whether I should have chosen something else. If I had more time with the menu, perhaps I would have been more confident in my choice. Maybe I should have involved my wife to have been more certain? Surely the waiter could have offered a greater endorsement for one dish or another? Back and forth the pendulum swings as my inner turmoil boils over with angst about the multitude of choices I have to select from and the possibility that I might not get it right.

Simply put, Cheesecake Factory makes my head hurt. They boast on their website that they make 250 menu items from scratch daily. But they also make it too difficult for me to select a meal and to feel good about my choice. This phenomenon is called the paradox of choice. We need choices, we need to feel that we are in control of our destiny—even in the case of a seemingly simple decision, like selecting a meal in a restaurant. When we are given too many options, however, a decision can become almost impossible to make. We occasionally manage to bungle through, but such experiences are rarely pleasant and frequently unfulfilling.

Shu and Carlson wrote in the *Journal of Marketing*, in an article titled "When Three Charms but Four Alarms: Identifying the Optimal Number of Claims in Persuasive Settings," "In several experiments, people were most receptive to a sales pitch for a product—whether it was a cereal, shampoo, restaurant, date, or politician—when presented with three selling points. Beyond three, skepticism increased markedly."

Unlike in a restaurant, where we are compelled to select something, a similar scenario in a retail store very often produces different results. Presenting too much information, and too many product options, can overwhelm the customer to the point that inaction becomes not just the preferred option but, in many cases, the only viable option.

When faced with a Cheesecake Factory–style portfolio of choices, too many customers leave the store without making any purchase at all. Their desire to escape the barrage of stuff (information and product) becomes far more enticing than their need to make a buying decision. They have become so overwhelmed with options that they experience buyer's paralysis, and removing themselves from that stress via leaving the store becomes the best course of action.

There is, of course, no absolute number of options that a customer should have in a retail store, but I believe that three is the right number once the conversation with the customer has advanced to the stage that product can be introduced. As Barry Schwartz wrote in *The Paradox of*

Choice, "Having the opportunity to choose is essential for well-being, but choice has negative features, and the negative features escalate as the number of choices increases."

As a point of clarification, my comments do not reflect a negative view of the Cheesecake Factory business model. It obviously works well for them, and the lines outside the door reflect very well on the overall experience and the quality of the food. I just don't like the stress of having to select from 250 menu items, and I choose to limit my visits for that reason.

Sonja Lyubomirsky writes in *The Myths of Happiness*:

One would think that having choices is desirable and advantageous—and it is, when the alternative is no choice. But possessing and combing through too many choices has now been persuasively shown by scientists to be toxic, because an inability to manage too many choices produces significant regret. When asked, most people declare that they prefer to have more rather than fewer options, whether they are choosing jobs, romantic partners, radio stations, or ice cream flavors. However, after the act of choosing is over—after we gamble on job A or groom B or sound system C—those of us who had more to choose from are less satisfied and, ultimately, much more likely to experience regret.

Limit the options you present to no more than three. There is a reason for that in as much as it satisfies our *need* to have choices without the added stress of having too many of them. This dictum applies to both products and information. If you are making your living in retail sales you will no doubt have experienced any number of occasions when a customer walked out without buying anything, leaving you wondering what else you could have done. It may not have been that you gave them too few choices and too little information. You may, in fact, have given them entirely too many options and an unnecessary overload of product facts and data.

Consider giving them three important pieces of information that you think might be relevant to them. If you do that, along with asking open-ended questions and doing a great job listening to their words and observing their body language, you will have given yourself every opportunity to make the sale. More often than you could ever imagine, and especially in sales, less is definitely more.

Contrast Principle

The contrast principle (sometimes called *anchoring*) suggests that it is always more beneficial to show your more expensive item first. That item, of course, should be positioned with one or two other options (as discussed in the previous chapter, I prefer three), and the items should be selected based on what you have learned from your active listening and from your open-ended questioning throughout the discovery process with your customer.

After you have established a nice rapport with your customer and you have worked together to narrow the choices, present three options. Each, of course, must meet the requirements uncovered in your conversation, and each item ought to be viable in and of itself. If the customer indicated that her preferred price is in the $5,000 range, I would present three options at $5,000, $7,500, and one in the $10,000 range.

Again, all three options should reflect the customer's feedback to your open-ended questions. The highest price serves as a psychological anchor that frames the other two options in a much more affordable light. There are multiple principles in play here; with the first option, the customer is being given ownership, rather than being told what to buy. He or she can feel as though they are driving the process of selection, even as they want the salesperson to drive the conversation.

With the second option, the salesperson is showing respect for the customer by including an option in his or her stated price range, because to do otherwise would create a real sense that it is the salesperson's agenda that is being played out, not the customer's. Once the customer offers a price range, it isn't a good idea not to include that as one of the three options.

And with the third option, the customer is gaining an entirely different perspective on relative value than if she had just been presented with one item—or multiple items of similar price—to select from. By presenting a higher-priced option (the anchor price), the requested price point looks much more affordable in contrast. A second price point, positioned between the lowest and highest price points, allows for an unconscious reframing of the customer's expectations. She will have been presented with an aspirational but accessible option that more often than not becomes the selected choice. Positioned between what she thought she wanted and what can appear to be just too much of a stretch, the middle option can look very appealing.

Barry Schwartz wrote about the principle of anchoring in *The Paradox of Choice*:

> One high-end catalog seller of mostly kitchen equipment and gourmet foods offered an automatic bread maker for $279. Sometime later, the catalog began to offer a larger capacity, deluxe version for $429. They didn't sell too many of these expensive bread makers, but sales of the less expensive one almost doubled! With the expensive bread maker serving as an anchor, the $279 machine had become a bargain.

Once again, adhering to the principles discussed in the previous chapter on the paradox of choice, and combining them with the contrast principle (anchoring) can be a hugely effective way to deliver just the right number of options to your customer—and in a way that invites that customer to comfortably reach beyond where she otherwise might have gone.

Daniel Kahneman, the Pulitzer Prize–winning economist and noted social psychologist, wrote in *Thinking, Fast and Slow*:

The anchoring effect is not a laboratory curiosity; it can be just as strong in the real world. In an experiment conducted some years ago, real-estate agents were given an opportunity to assess the value of a house that was actually on the market. They visited the house and studied a comprehensive booklet of information that included an asking price. Half the agents saw an asking price that was substantially higher than the listed price of the house; the other half saw an asking price that was substantially lower. Each agent gave her opinion about a reasonable buying price for the house and the lowest price at which she would agree to sell the house if she owned it. The agents were then asked about the factors that had affected their judgment. Remarkably, the asking price was not one of these factors; the agents took pride in their ability to ignore it. They insisted that the listing price had no effect on their responses, but they were wrong; the anchoring effect was 41%. Indeed, the professionals were almost as susceptible to anchoring effects as business school students with no real-estate experience, whose anchoring was 48%. The only difference between the two groups was that the students conceded that they were influenced by the anchor, while the professionals denied that influence.

In the three price examples that we used in this chapter, $5,000, $7,500, and $10,000, studies suggest that the customer will generally select the middle option—in this example, $7,500. It is priced well enough to be realistically accessible, relative to where the customer stated she wanted to be ($5,000), and yet it appears to be a very good price relative to the anchor price ($10,000).

A salesperson who can successfully incorporate the contrast principle into their regular routine would likely see a vast increase in their own sales productivity. While the research shows that a large majority of customers select the middle option, even a small number opting for the middle price can deliver as much as a 50 percent increase in average sales ticket for each successful transaction. It doesn't take Daniel Kahneman to figure out what that can do for your sales over the course of a given month or year.

Once when I was conducting a training session at a jewelry store in Michigan, we got talking about the paradox of choice and the contrast principle. The team seemed to welcome and grasp the concepts, and as a pragmatic way of combining the two principles, and incorporating a new idea of product information and learning, I challenged the team to do the following: I suggested that they select three items from their inventory that could be used to accomplish the two principles. For instance, three diamond pendants priced at $3,000, $5,000, and $7,000 would do the trick. Or indeed any combination of three items that might be enticing for someone looking to buy a special gift. I suggested that they pre-select the items and become familiar with them so that they could be used at the appropriate time with a customer. Once they understood the value of doing that preparation, I then recommended that they do ten different versions of that mini-story. That might include three engagement rings, three timepieces, three pairs of earrings, or just about any combination to reflect the idea of three options at three different price points.

Doing this takes work. It should not be a mindless task that can whipped through in an hour; it can and should be a learned discipline that evolves as the product dynamic changes on the sales floor. It is not for the lazy, for sales "clerks," or for those people who see sales as beneath them.

Once the groundwork has been done, an exercise like this can be a very powerful tool to help a customer. It doesn't, of course, mean that the customer will select only from those ten stories (thirty items), but it gives him or her a nice range of choices and price-points, and it can serve as a great roadmap to uncovering the customer's needs and quickly establishing a rapport.

Eliel Garcia sat through one of my trainings a while back, and mere minutes after the training ended, he welcomed a customer who entered his store. The customer produced a plain gold band and indicated that he was in the market for a diamond that his girlfriend could wear with the band. After Eliel spent some time getting to know his customer and learning as much as he could about his girlfriend, he checked with his jeweler to determine how much the work would cost to turn the gold band into a semi-mounting to accommodate a diamond.

Once that cost was established, Eliel worked with the customer to determine what his budget was, and when he learned it was $3,000, he decided to apply the teaching from his still-fresh training on the paradox of choice and the contrast principle. He presented three diamonds using the customer's budget as the baseline. After some exceptionally effective team-selling with his colleague Tiffany, who had suggested the customer view the diamond outside the store in the natural light, the customer opted for a diamond that would cost him $4600 when materials and labor were combined.

Eliel had brilliantly executed the paradox of choice and the contrast principle, and a sale that looked like it might be in $3,000 range ended up being greater than 50 percent higher because Eliel and Tiffany used their training on the two principles, combined with their own very effective team-selling standards.

Eliel said that the customer left his store absolutely satisfied with his purchase and feeling quite certain that the diamond he purchased was going to delight his fiancé and make both of them extremely proud. He was also, according to Eliel, thrilled that he was not going to have to visit multiple jewelry stores to take care of his needs. A win-win all around. My abiding memory of the visit is Tiffany, his colleague, tapping me on the shoulder and saying, "It worked. Eliel just used it, and it worked."

Losing Feels Worse Than Winning Feels Great

*"I wanted to leave a mark on the world. I wanted to win.
No, that's not right. I simply didn't want to lose."*

—PHIL KNIGHT

I was watching an English Premier League soccer game on television last year between struggling Newcastle United and the then champions, Chelsea. Despite the fact that it was only the seventh game of the thirty-eight-game season, a certain pattern was already emerging for the home team, Newcastle. They had not won a single game up to that point, and they already seemed destined for another season of struggle, as they attempted to maintain their spot in the top division. Somehow, in one of the great mysteries of the "beautiful game," Newcastle found themselves leading Chelsea 2–0 late in the game. In a late flurry by the champions, however, Chelsea scored two goals to tie the match and threatened to destroy the good work that Newcastle had done up to that point.

What really caught my attention in the midst of the drama was a decision the Newcastle team made with less than a minute remaining in the game. They were awarded a corner kick, and rather than view it as an opportunity to drive the ball into Chelsea's penalty box in an attempt to score the winning goal and win the match, they chose to take a short corner and use the remaining time in the game, content to preserve the point they had by aimlessly passing the ball.

To put that strategy into context, what the Newcastle players and coaches were doing was settling for the one point that a tie would have provided instead of trying to win the three points that they would have been awarded for a win. In short, the threat of *losing* a single point was a much greater motivator than the possibility of actually winning three points.

The logic—or lack thereof—of Newcastle's choice to play for one point instead of three can only be understood when one considers the tiny margins that often separate the teams in the Premier League, the top division, from teams in the second tier each year.

In eight of the last ten years, the difference between the third-worst team at season's end (relegated to the second tier along with the two teams below them) and the fourth-worst team (allowed to remain in the Premier League) has been three points or less. There were five years where the difference was one point or less. With that kind of history, Newcastle should have taken a chance to secure the extra two points, the difference between a win and a tie.

For a team seemingly destined to struggle at the bottom of the league table, that corner kick represented a precious opportunity to try to win the game, and yet Newcastle folded their tent to protect the one point they had. Not losing that point was a much stronger motivator than winning three points.

Finishing in the bottom three places and getting relegated to the second tier of English soccer can cost a soccer club hundreds of millions of dollars in lost revenue. Further, falling into the lower division does not bring with it any promise of temporary residence. It can be the beginning of a decade or more of decline that can devastate a club and destroy the hopes of its fan base—and negatively impact the community itself.

For example, Leeds United was once one of the most storied teams in the world, and they have since fallen into chronic disrepair. Other teams such as Wigan, Wolves, and Portsmouth are all in various states of difficulty after they too suffered relegation. Their fans went from watching Liverpool, Manchester United, and Arsenal in their home stadiums to seeing much less glamorous teams in games with decidedly less glamor. The system of relegation and promotion in the soccer leagues in Europe makes for compelling watching and great drama. It is, however, utterly devastating to the fan bases, clubs, and communities when their team suffers relegation. Can you imagine the Yankees and Red Sox getting relegated to Triple-A baseball?

As I watched the Newcastle versus Chelsea game, I was reminded that logic alone is rarely an important enough motivator. We are much more motivated to *not lose* something than we are to *gain* something. It is an important psychological factor, and recognizing it as such can be very powerful in understanding human behavior. While many companies build their sales and advertising efforts around the idea of what we gain by buying something—she will have better skin if she uses brand X, he will be a hero if he buys brand Y—what the coach of Newcastle United demonstrated was that he was far less motivated to come out a hero, as would have been the case if his team had defeated Chelsea, than he was to not look like a chump by losing after his team had been leading by 2–0.[1] As it happens, not looking like a chump is a major motivator, and the sooner we understand that, the better we will be able to maximize our sales opportunities.

Robert Cialdini wrote in *Influence: The Psychology of Persuasion*, "The idea of potential loss plays a large role in human decision-making. In fact, people seem more motivated by the thought of losing something than they do by the thought of gaining something of equal value."

Immediately after I wrote the first draft of this chapter, I went for a long walk with my then fourteen-year-old son. I was talking to him about

---

1 Newcastle United was relegated from the Premier League at the end of that season and will now play in the decidedly less glamorous second tier of English football. Instead of playing the top teams in the country, they must now resign themselves to the task of attempting to win promotion back into the Premier League. There is no guarantee that it will happen anytime soon or at all. They were relegated by two points.

my observation in the Newcastle versus Chelsea game, and I asked him what he thought about the idea that we are more motivated to avoid loss than we are to realize a gain. We chatted for a while, and I then asked him to think about an example in his life, the school dance, to see how it worked in his world. I asked him to consider what his real motivation was when he got dressed for a dance. I asked him if he thought that impressing the girls was more of a driver than *not looking bad* to those same girls. Without hesitation, he said that not looking bad was a much more powerful motivator than actually looking like the cool dude at the dance.

What I saw in the soccer match, and what my son had shared with me in his example, was living proof of what Sheena Iyengar wrote in her book, *The Art of Choosing*: "We do whatever we can to avoid losing the things that are most important to us, but we don't take similar risks to achieve gains because we worry that we might incur a loss instead."

Bart Marks, a great salesman in his own right, shared the following story with me:

> One point I have always emphasized with my sales team is that it is their jobs to influence the customers, not just to inform and offer product information. I regularly challenge them to think of their very best customers, the ones who love us, who come to all of our events and who bake us cakes and goodies for Christmas. What do they all have in common? Well, for one thing, the chances are pretty good that they spend much more in our store than they ever intend to; they listen to us; they take our advice. Customers who buy on price alone don't love us. They have no loyalty to our brand or to our store whatsoever.
>
> There's an interesting irony that plays out in retail stores on a regular basis.
>
> Whenever a new prospect visits the store and is very *specific* about what they want, our sales champions know that the best opportunities lie in selling them something *different* than what they asked for. That is, I confess, counterintuitive (let's give the

customer what they want and all that mumbo-jumbo), but we usually have better success by parking the specific request away in the recesses of our mind and focusing on inspiring the customer to want something *even better* than they had asked for.

One of the main reasons is that adhering very specifically, and quite literally, to the initial request means that we are really in a price conversation, as the customer's specificity was clearly seeded someplace else, long before they entered our store. That means we are probably competing with some other store or online site in a race to the bottom.

The second reason we believe we need to sell them something better is because our culture is deeply rooted in the belief that it is our responsibility as sales professionals to inspire and influence the customer to aspire to something better, not settle for the lowest price and the lowest common denominator. For instance, Susan, in our Reno store, recently greeted a customer (with a friend/adviser in tow), and the following conversation ensued:

"I want the biggest diamond I can buy for $3000, and I don't really care about quality."

"Certainly," Susan replied, as she led him to the diamond case and found a .85ct solitaire diamond to show to him. The diamond was promotional quality (more about price than quality), but it met the customer's price requirement.

The diamond was good value for the money, but Susan knew it was likely no better than many of the other diamonds the customer and his friend would have seen that day in their travels. She knew that would have to do more to earn his business.

Susan gave him a minute with the diamond and then said, "Look, I know this isn't really what you asked for, but there's something I want you to see." She reached into another part of the showcase and produced a .62ct branded diamond that was clearly a much better quality.

"It's very pretty," he acknowledged, *"but I really wanted something bigger."*

"Wait right here," Susan replied, and she then proceeded to walk to the other side of the store, holding both items aloft as she did so. *"Which one sparkles more?"* she asked.

Both the customer and his friend readily acknowledged that the branded diamond sparkled more—*much more.*

"How far do you think I am from you right now?" Susan asked.

"Twenty-five feet," he guessed.

"Is that big enough?" she asked. *"Light travels,"* she continued. *"That's what people see. That's what's going to make people stop your fiancée to tell her how beautiful her diamond is."*

By focusing on advantages and benefits, rather than features, Susan had helped the customer to appreciate that he needed something different, something better, than he had originally requested.

"You've made your point," he said, *"but I made up my mind that I am not spending any more than $3000 on the diamond."* The branded diamond was not only smaller, it was also $500 more.

"I get it," Susan responded. *"You could settle for the $3000 diamond, but before you do, you might ask yourself this question: Did you save $500, or did you waste $3000, because you didn't get the diamond you really wanted?"*

The fear of losing something is far greater than the desire for gain. The customer paid the extra money for the branded diamond, plus a few hundred dollars more for a solitaire setting and tax. His desire to adhere to a given budget was no match for his desire to *not do the wrong thing.* He could have bought the larger, lesser-quality diamond, but Susan inspired him to a better solution for him and for his intended.

Some weeks later, Susan received a photo from him that showed him proposing to his girlfriend. They have both thanked her for helping him to buy such a beautiful diamond, and they have expressed gratitude and loyalty by suggesting that they would never again consider shopping in another jewelry store.

Freeman Hall, who wrote a very funny book called *Retail Hell* about his experience working for Nordstrom, or "The Big Fancy," as he called it in the book, described the following situation:

"Are you done with this?'" I asked, reaching for the suede bag. "My customer would like to see it." As the words came out of my mouth, I knew that I'd made a critical mistake. I felt like a zombie, so I wasn't thinking clearly. What can I say? From experience, I knew what was going to happen next. You see, whenever there is only one left of something on sale, and two women suddenly start eyeing it for whatever reason, the one that picks it up first wins. And even though the winner may not really want it, if she's a bitch, she'll buy it out of spite, just to keep the other one from having it. It's a common occurrence in Handbag Jungle.

The idea of losing that handbag is no different than the scenario we often see play out in auctions when two or more people become fixated on becoming the successful bidder. They are not so much competing to buy the item in question as they are bidding to avoid losing.

So, how do you introduce this concept into your language without sounding negative? It certainly wouldn't do to tell customers that they are making a mistake by buying item A versus item B. They won't respond to your suggesting that they have bad taste or that they're headed down the wrong path with a particular purchase. In short, your objective should be to have specific phrases that you can use at the appropriate time that speak to the customer's unconscious desire to *avoid* doing the wrong thing.

For instance, try using a very quiet: "This is a great choice, and you won't regret buying this particular piece." That comment serves two purposes: it reinforces the customer's instinct, if he or she was heading in that direction, and it subtly underscores the importance *not making the wrong choice.*

Another similar example that you could use is, "Look, I'm sure you would like her to enjoy this for many years to come. You will not have to second-guess this choice." Once again, you are complimenting your customer's good taste (even if he or she was less than certain up to that point) and reminding them that they just don't want to do the wrong thing.

As Zig Ziglar wrote in *Closing the Sale*, "It's a psychological fact that the fear of loss is greater than the desire for gain."

Discounting

"Long-term greedy is better than short-term greedy."

—Warren Buffett

There is a certain myth in my industry that suggests a salesperson who writes a million dollars of business a year is to be celebrated, coveted, and, if they work for someone else, recruited. There are, of course, many fine examples of the aforementioned salespeople who are in fact at the very top of their game and who should be acknowledged and rewarded accordingly. Unfortunately, there are also a great many salespeople who believe—and lead their managers to believe—they are great because they write a million dollars in business but who are, in some cases, also killing the business.

They are "successful" because they place a huge premium on generating top-line sales, with little to no consideration for whether those sales produce appropriate margins or are, in the most extreme cases, even profitable. Of course, if you happen to work for a retail store that encourages discounting, perhaps one that even builds its marketing around being off-price, ignore this section completely and skip to the next chapter.

Martin Lindstrom wrote in *Buyology: Truth and Lies About Why We Buy:*

Let's say you bought a Ralph Lauren shirt today at 70 percent discount. In two years from now, when things go more or less back to normal, would you even consider buying that same shirt at full price? You wouldn't—because your brain expects that low price. In fact, for years I've been telling my clients around the world that studies show it takes seven years for a brand to recover its value in the minds of consumers once it's been discounted. Seven years!

Whether you are a branded environment or a largely unbranded environment, it is worth heeding Lindstrom's warning. The allure of discounting is very appealing in the moment. We are all anxious to make the sale, and, consciously or otherwise, we want to be perceived well by our customers. Discounting can appear to be a way to accomplish both objectives, but it comes at a heavy cost.

The most obvious cost to the business is that every dollar of discount means less profit to the store. There is—and unfortunately this is not always as transparent as it should be—a fine line after which a sale becomes bad business.

A second issue is one of credibility and believability. No matter how deeply you discount, the customer will rarely ever be certain that he or she got the best deal. That uncertainty can erode confidence in the store and in the salesperson, and detract from the experience of buying something that should have made them feel great.

A third issue is one of loyalty or, more to the point, a lack thereof. If you "win" a sale on the strength of discounting, it is very likely that the customer will feel no sense of loyalty to you or to the store. She may actually be so sufficiently seduced by the discount game that she will continue to play it with your store and others thereafter.

And the worst of all possibilities is that she *continues* to frequent your place of business but never allows your store to make a profit on her purchases. One of the hardest things to do in business is to fire employees. Even more difficult than that is to fire customers. If your discounting becomes a crutch for you (you just can't seem to sell without it) and a drug for your customer, you may be headed for a perfect storm that will sink your boat for good.

Daniel Kahneman wrote in his book *Thinking, Fast and Slow*:

> People who learned from a new catalog that the merchant was now charging less for a product that they had recently bought at a higher price reduced their future purchases from that supplier by 15%, an average loss of $90 per customer. The customer evidently perceived the lower price as the reference point and thought of themselves as having sustained a loss by paying more than appropriate.

High sales producers who frequently practice discounting are not the good salespeople they would have you believe. They consistently show an inability to inspire and influence the customer's behavior by establishing a value proposition for the product and/or service, and they often overshadow the real star performers, who don't always scale the heights of top-line sales but who produce very credible numbers, while still maintaining a healthy profit margin for the business.

Raynor and Ahmed wrote in *The Three Rules: How Exceptional Companies Think*:

> There are two dimensions of value along which any company can differentiate itself: price value and non-price value. Our research reveals that exceptional companies typically focus on price value, even if that means they have to charge higher prices. It did not have to turn out this way: price-based competition is a legitimate strategy. We have found, however, that competing with *better* rather than cheaper is systematically associated with superior, long-term performance.

The last point I will make on discounting is that if you must do it, *use dollars not percentages*. Customers don't spend or save percentages. They don't fill their gas tank using percentages, and they don't get paid in percentages. It is so easy to throw around terms such as 10 percent off, or 20 percent off, as if they have no meaning or cost to the business. Before you know it, you've "offed" your profitability.

If you must give a discount, talk in dollars. It's what we earn, it's what we spend, and it's what we know. If you are selling something for a thousand dollars, and you offer the customer a 15 percent discount, it may actually mean less than if you offered a one-hundred-dollar price consideration. Enough of those fifty-dollar savings can make or break a business in the course of a year. Eddy Kay wrote in *Thriving in the Shadow of Giants*, "Without seeing the value in a product, the price will always be expensive."

Value and price are entirely different propositions, and salespeople who believe they are providing great value to their customers and to their businesses by offering regular discounts are deluding themselves. Unless your business is working on an extremely low overhead—and if it is, please drop me a line about how to afford to pay a great sales team in that scenario!— you cannot survive with a discounting mentality. Instead, you need to identify and communicate your value proposition and expect more from your clients. They just might surprise you.

Permission to Buy

"Would we have bought that chair if she had asked us?"

—Sherry Smith

My wife and I redid our home office some months ago, and we decided to buy a chair to help create a nice reading retreat. Occasionally, one of us wants to retire to a quiet, comfortable space and lose ourselves in a book, escaping the general hustle and bustle from a house full of teenagers.

We went to our local Pier 1 store and immediately spotted a wonderful little chair that looked like it might suit our purposes. I took the chair down from an elevated platform, and my wife and I took turns test-driving it to make sure it would work for us. After a quick walk around the store to ensure there was not a better option, we returned to the chair, and we were eventually approached by a salesperson who asked us if we needed any help.

We let her know that we were interested in the chair, and she went away to check on its availability. While she was away, we noticed that there was a small chip on one of the legs. It was not a major concern to us, but it was certainly noticeable. When the salesperson returned, she announced that this particular chair was out of stock but that they expected more to arrive in the next two or three weeks. She added that we could take the sample if we wanted.

We pointed out that there was a slight chip in one of the legs and, without us having asked for one, she said, "We don't discount."

She then turned and walked away without another word from her or from us and did not return to engage us in any way. We looked at each other as if to say, "Did that really happen?"

There were any number of things that salesperson might have done to close the sale. She could have assumed the sale and asked for our information so she could contact us as soon as a new chair came in. She could have pointed out that the little chip was very minor and would easily be masked with a furniture pen. Or she might have downplayed the chip, while still offering to see if her manager would make a small price adjustment as a gesture.

Without a shadow of doubt, any of the aforementioned options would have resulted in us buying the chair that day, resulting in a $500 sale for Pier 1, a company, perhaps unsurprisingly, that has seen its stock in free fall for the last few years. My wife and I left the store without the chair, shaking our heads at the complete indifference, incompetence, and, quite frankly, the ignorance of that particular salesperson.

We wondered how many times a day situations like that happened in that store and what the impact was on their sales results over the course of a week, a month, a year. The salesperson had expected the least of us, and she had successfully orchestrated her self-fulfilling prophecy. As the late Herb Greenberg often said, "You can teach skills, you cannot teach attitude and motivation." All we needed was permission to buy that chair, and she never gave it to us.

My friend Rich Pesqueira shared the following story with me:

As a customer, I honestly believe the very best service a salesperson can give me is to offer an idea that is better than what I originally might have had in mind when I came into the store. All too often, the problem-solving responsibility falls on the customer's shoulders, under the guise of "polite service," when, in fact, it is really more about the salesperson not owning the process.

I had occasion to make multiple visits to a popular guitar store that provided generally good service experiences, but no end result. I had made a promise to myself that if my sales team hit certain targets for the year, I would treat myself to a new guitar. I already had a perfectly good one that had cost me about $300, but I wanted to spoil myself with something that thirty years from now would still remind me of this important time in my life.

After managing to scrape and claw our way to the needed year-end results, I set off for the guitar store with a spring in my step and money burning a hole in my pocket.

When I entered the store, I was greeted by a friendly sales-man, who proceeded to give me a master class in safe and, unfortunately, uninspiring service:

"Hello, can I help you?"

"Hi . . . I am thinking about buying myself a new guitar."

"Great, acoustic or electric?"

"Acoustic."

"Steel-string or nylon?"

"Steel."

"What brands are you considering?"

"I was thinking maybe a Taylor or a Gibson."

"How much do you want to spend?"

"I don't know, maybe $1500?"

"Great, come with me."

Off we went across the store, and the salesman showed me a few guitars based on my answers to his basic questions. With a built-in seek-and-destroy shopping mentality and a healthy dose of buyer's motivation, I nonetheless found myself generally uninspired and, quite frankly, ambivalent about what I was seeing. The friendly clerk encouraged me to take my time (there was my get-out-of-jail-free card) and eventually ambled off, leaving me alone to contemplate the guitars. After a few minutes, I decided that I just wasn't in the mood to make a buying decision, and I left the store empty-handed and a little frustrated. Ironically, I was satisfied with the service I'd received from the salesman but disappointed that I had not been inspired to make a purchase.

Despite really wanting to treat myself to a new guitar, I became distracted by a million other demands, and I didn't go back to the guitar store until about six weeks later. Much to my chagrin, I had the same experience again, albeit it with a different salesperson. In fact, on several subsequent visits over the coming months, I was subjected to variations of the same theme, all ending the same way; me leaving the store without a new guitar.

Many weeks later, I returned once more to the store and met a salesman named Jeff.

"Hey! How are you doing today?"

"Good, you?"

"Super."

"What brings you in today?"

"I've been thinking about getting a new guitar."

"That's exciting. What do you play now?"

"I have a Yamaha acoustic I bought from you as a starter guitar a few years ago. I paid about $300 for it."

"They do a great job for the money. What made you decide on a new guitar?"

"Well, I had a big year at work and I promised myself a reward."

"Awesome. Congratulations! Now, of all the things you could have bought, why a new guitar?"

"Well, I wanted something really special that I'll have forever, something I wouldn't normally do for myself. I want something tangible to remember an exciting time in my life."

"I totally get it. Tell me, what is important to you about the guitar you choose?"

I hadn't really thought about this until he asked, but I suddenly had some clarity,

"I want it to sound noticeably different than ordinary guitars. I want to almost hear angels sing when I play it. I want it to be aesthetically beautiful and, if I'm being really honest, when other musicians see it, I want them to raise an eyebrow and think, *Wow, that's a great guitar.*"

After asking me a few questions about what I consider a beautiful, rich sound, he said

"I get it; I know what you should see!"

He then showed me a few really special guitars. He had me play them, and, as I did so, he pointed out specific features and taught me how to hear the different tones created by exceptional guitars. He then took each guitar from me and played it himself (with amazing skill) so I could hear how other people would experience it when I'm playing (cue the laugh track . . .).

Jeff got a little feedback from me, and he then picked up a beautiful Martin D35E Retro and pointed out that it had everything that was important to me in a guitar. It was also $3500. I was a little uneasy, because it was almost two and a half times what I had "decided" to spend and, more importantly, what I had told my wife I would spend.

He told me, with absolute conviction, that what I really wanted in a guitar would cost $3500. He reminded me that I had stated that I wanted to remember this time in my life by doing something special for myself. He also told me that if I didn't do it now, it would be very easy to talk myself out of it. He said I deserved it and that if I took it home and my wife disagreed, to bring it back. I gave him my credit card.

Every night when I see that guitar on the stand in my living room, I proudly pick it up and play a little. It is like a warm hug to me, and it is always one of my favorite times of the day. Jeff changed my life by looking beyond my basic feedback, and by mining beneath the exterior to understand what my real motivations were. I know now that I was never going to buy a $1500 guitar—no matter how politely the other employees followed my instructions. I mean, I was the customer, and isn't the customer always right?

Martin Lindstrom wrote in his wonderful book, *Buyology: Truth and Lies about Why We Buy*, "As we have seen again and again, most of our buying decisions aren't remotely conscious. Our brain makes the decision and most of the time we aren't even aware of it."

Salespeople, even some capable salespeople, make the mistake of believing the first thing that comes out of the customer's mouth, and they skip off down the yellow-brick road in the naive belief that they are serving the customer best by believing that he or she has it all figured out prior to visiting the store.

There are obviously occasions when a customer *does* know what he or she wants, but that isn't often the case. Encountering a customer who is unable to articulate their needs, or, as in Rich's case, someone who has a false sense of what his needs *really* are, is where great experiences happen and great salespeople succeed.

Rich has the guitar he didn't even know he wanted, and it took months of experiencing adequate but uninspiring service before he finally met a great salesperson who gave him permission to buy. The guitar store had managed to beat the odds and enjoyed the loyalty of a customer who had failed to be inspired on multiple previous visits and who still returned again and again. It is more typical to get one chance with a customer.

Jonah Berger wrote in *Contagious: Why Things Catch On*, "Rather than harping on features of facts, we need to focus on feelings: the underlying emotions that motivate people to action." Rich stayed with the guitar store long enough to be finally rewarded with the permission slip he so long desired, without even really knowing it. His experiences were a wonderful reminder of how the best salespeople can inspire action and give permission to the customer to extend themselves into places they never knew they wanted to go.

Closing

"The hard part about a novel is to finish it."

—ERNEST HEMINGWAY

I'm sure that at some point or other in the course of your career you have heard the term *assumptive close*. What that means exactly is subject to interpretation, and I suspect that one could offer a sound argument as to whether the term itself is actually viable. In its most literal meaning, it implies that you should assume the close after you have worked through the selling process. Under this assumption, act like you will get the sale and it should happen, right?

Of course, what that assumption does not tell us is when in the sales process you should act like you have earned the close. What if you didn't do a very good job in working to uncover the customer's needs or wants? Perhaps you get to the part where you expect and/or ask the all-important question, and you find out that the customer doesn't share your assessment of you needing to close and them needing to buy.

I won't pretend to know the exact moment when a sale has been earned and a salesperson should attempt to close the customer, but what I will say is that you had better go into every customer interaction with the expectation that you will get there sooner or later. And, recognizing the premium we place on our time nowadays, it ought to be sooner more often than later.

Of course, the assumption I will make is that you have done a good job in the time leading up to asking for the sale and that, to paraphrase the old Smith Barney commercial, you have "earned it."

I have heard from people who believe a salesperson ought to ask for the sale in every single transaction. Beyond the obvious repair, returns, or service interactions that may not provide that opportunity, such a mandate is a little bit like throwing stuff at the wall. You have to have arrived at the point in your conversation with the customer where asking for the sale is an obvious next step. If you haven't done your job engaging the customer—asking relevant open-ended questions and listening to what he or she is telling you—then your attempts to close the sale will be nothing more than an academic exercise, with precious little relevance to the situation you might find yourself in.

So as not to confuse the reader, I should state that I am unapologetically, categorically, and most passionately an advocate of asking for the sale in the vast majority of customer interactions—and I believe that doing so is one of the most underutilized disciplines in most sales environments. All too often we see sales clerks—and I use the term *clerks* quite deliberately here—standing behind the counter waiting for the customer to make a decision. I have personally had experiences with sales clerks who would sooner assume the fetal position and cry their eyes out than ask the dreaded question. They seem to do everything but ask for the sale, piling on ever more product information, flashing uncomfortable and nervous smiles, fidgeting and engaging in other distracting behaviors—almost begging someone to come and rescue them.

These kinds of salespeople are, at their core, Monopoly players, dispensing get-out-of-jail-free cards designed to allow their customers to pass Go so that they can find another salesperson in another store to close them. They are the kind of salespeople who tell their managers they're sure that customer will return—they just need to think on it for a while. They just have a gut feeling, they'll tell you, blissfully unaware that they've lost the opportunity to make the sale and to satisfy a potential customer, who actually took the time to visit their store for a reason.

The challenges that ineffective salespeople have in closing sales begin long before the customer ever enters the store. They are deeply rooted in an unconscious delusion that customers don't actually *want* to make a purchase at all. That they do so only under great duress. They further believe that any attempt to overly influence the customer's decision-making is somehow immoral, a disruption of the natural order of things, where customers tell the salesperson what and when they are willing to buy, and any interference on the salesperson's part is, well, pushy.

Martin Lindstrom wrote in *Buyology: Truth and Lies about Why We Buy*:

> When you see the shiny digital camera, or those flashy diamond earrings, for example, dopamine suddenly flushes your brain with pleasure, then wham, before you know it, you've signed the credit card receipt (researchers agree that it takes 2.5 seconds to make a purchasing decision).

Customers not only want to buy, but in many instances, they are physiologically wired to buy. Weak salespeople deny them the opportunity to fulfill that need by not assertively and confidently leading the conversation toward a purchasing decision. The first rule of closing is to accept unequivocally that every customer who visits your store is willing to make a purchase if you do your job properly.

The second rule is that you have an obligation to your customer, to your employer, and to yourself to ask for the sale with confidence and the expectation of a close. I am not suggesting that you subvert or shortcut the sales process and proceed straight to the close, but you must believe that the customer wants to buy and will buy, and you must ask for the sale when you have done your job. There will always be challenges to closing, and you will clearly not close 100 percent of your customers, but you can bet, as Wayne Gretzky famously said, you will miss 100 percent of the shots you do not take.

Jim Douglas, a very effective sales trainer in his own right, shared the following story with me about closing:

> During a sales training at a store, I covered the importance of discovery and how it can be applied throughout the presentation up to and including the close. In particular, I emphasized what I consider to be an absolute imperative for every salesperson when the customer breaks off the conversation with, "Let me think about that."
>
> The response I recommend in that situation is, "I understand, but I've found that could mean something about this isn't right. What about this might not be right?" Putting the emphasis on the word *might* takes the combativeness and pressure out of the equation and, in the vast majority of instances, shifts the conversation back to the customer.
>
> A short time after the training, I received a phone call from the manager of the store. He thought I would like to hear what happened. The newest sales associate in the store was working with a customer who was looking for a Christmas gift for his wife. She was showing him a diamond pendant that he seemed to be very interested in when, seemingly out of the blue, he said, "Let me think about that." With the training fresh in her mind, the salesperson looked at him and said, "I totally understand, but I've found that could mean something about this particular pendant just isn't right. What about this pendant might not be just right?" He looked at her and without skipping a beat said, "She likes yellow gold." The salesperson had been showing him a white-gold pendant, never thinking that he wanted yellow-gold. The manager said the associate let out a small gasp of release (realizing that her training was about to pay dividends) and said, "Oh, we have this pendant in yellow gold." The customer was delighted and the sale was made.

As obvious as it may have seemed to everyone else in the store, the customer didn't know that the pendant was also available in yellow gold, and he was about to leave the store instead of asking. A customer's reasons for not making a purchase don't have to be complex. It can be as simple as the above scenario, and a well-placed question can be the difference between making the sale and not making the sale, satisfying a customer, or leaving them empty-handed and frustrated.

It is worth pointing out that as frustrating as it is for a salesperson when a customer leaves the store empty-handed, it is also equally frustrating for the customer, who came into the store for something and yet ended up not satisfying their needs.

Another psychological factor in helping to close the sale is the customer's inherent desire to act immediately. This desire can be subconscious, but make no mistake, it can be very present, even if it is not articulated. If you can create an emotional bond with the customer and you have reasonably determined that you have arrived at an appropriate solution, then you will be doing all parties a favor by bringing the conversation to a satisfactory resolution. Remember, you have now committed to believing that all customers come into your store to make a purchase, so get it done. Ask for the sale, and do so with confidence and with very positive body language.

As Martin Lindstrom wrote:

The psychologists asked a group of random students to choose between a pair of Amazon.com gift vouchers. If they picked the first, a $15 gift voucher, they would get it at once. If they were willing to wait two weeks for the $20 gift certificate, well, obviously they'd be getting more bang for their buck. The brain scans revealed that both gift options triggered activity in the lateral prefrontal cortex, the area of the brain that generates emotion. But the possibility of getting that $15 gift certificate *now* caused an unusual flurry of stimulation in the limbic area of most students' brains—a whole grouping of brain structures that's primarily responsible for our emotional life, as well as for the formation of memory. The more the students were emotionally excited about something, the psychologists found, the greater the chances of opting for the immediate, if less immediately gratifying, alternative. Of course, their rational minds knew the $20 was logically a better deal, but—guess what—their emotions won out.

Of course the customer can continue to shop and potentially return to your store. It happens from time to time. On the other hand, if you believe that the customer will buy today, if you conduct yourself accordingly, and if you *ask* for the sale when you have earned that right, everyone wins. Nathan Jamail wrote in *The Sales Professionals Playbook*, "Closing a sale is straightforward, and like most things in sales, it is a simple concept, but not necessarily easy to do. We don't want to be pushy, yet at the same time we need to ask for the business." Not doing so is a disservice to the customer, the store, and the salesperson.

Client Development

"Loyalty is when people are willing to turn down a better product or a better price to continue doing business with you."

—SIMON SINEK

I love Amazon and eBay because they get me. Okay, you're right, they don't actually get me. In fact, they don't even know me. That said, their algorithms really get me, and they make my online shopping experiences so much easier. They have captured my purchasing and browsing history, and they seem to know just what to serve up and when. For their efforts, I frequently reward both sites with purchases that I had no idea I wanted or needed and that, to be honest, I was only too happy to make.

I'll buy another book and stack it on top of the other two hundred books waiting to be read, or another Frank Sinatra or Nat King Cole collectible for that jazz club that I am working on for my retirement, or a signed photo of a Liverpool player, circa the 1970s. The point is, because I have a purchasing history, I am not only fair game for follow-up purchases, I am unconsciously looking to make them when I sign on to those sites. I'm always excited by what might be suggested for me, and the experience is almost like a great trip to the Brimfield Antique Market in

Western Massachusetts—filled with promise, entirely disorganized, but beautifully rewarding.

Now, let me tell you about the last time I got a note or an email from anyone in a brick-and-mortar store. Okay, so there isn't anything to tell. Even in my world, where I unconsciously seek out retail experiences, I cannot remember the last time I got a note or an email from anyone.

To be fair, I have recently received a couple of calls from my salesperson at Ethan Allen, but I'm reluctant to give her too much credit as I expect her attention has been fueled by a conversation I had with her manager. A few weeks ago, with my wife and son, we went into the store one Saturday. Within a few minutes of entering, Dolores had welcomed us and already secured my name, phone number, and email. Impressive, right?

We told Dolores that we were in the market for a couch and some chairs, and that we intended to visit a couple of other stores that day before finally making our decision. That said, we had readily given up our contact information, and we took the time to select a couch and three chairs that were of interest to us. We even went to the trouble of picking out the fabric for the various pieces in case we wanted to call back and place an order. We then left the store to continue our shopping.

As we were leaving, my wife and I talked about how impressed we were with Dolores, and we wondered what her follow-up would be. No one could have mistaken our visit for anything other than *motivated* and *serious*, and, to her credit, she had seamlessly and successfully secured all of my contact information. I anticipated an email or text later that day to thank us for coming in, and to see how the rest of our day's shopping went.

Saturday and Sunday passed without any contact, as did Monday and Tuesday. I finally went back to the store on Wednesday to order the furniture, and I asked for Dolores. I wanted to give her the order, as she had spent time with us when we were in, but I also wanted to ask her why she'd failed to follow up.

As it happened, she was not there because she had left on vacation. I sat down with her manager, and I told her that I wanted Dolores to get credit for the sale, but also that I was very surprised that she had not followed up. Even though the manager indicated that our salesperson had left for vacation, she agreed that there should have been some follow-up. The sale was for more than $6000, and, while Ethan Allen regularly makes such sales, something like that should have warranted a little more follow-through from the salesperson. We were motivated enough to buy, despite there being no contact post-visit, but that is clearly not always the case when customers leave a store and the salesperson doesn't follow up.

I'm a guy that actually likes to shop—just ask my kids. Although they swear I only shop so I can make notes about my experiences with salespeople, that's not entirely true, but habits are hard to break, and I do use my phone to capture notes about particularly good or bad experiences. Dolores called and left a message thanking me for asking for her when we returned to make the purchase. She never did explain why she had failed to follow-up afterward.

I remember visiting a jewelry store in San Diego some years ago and being floored by the culture of client development. All of the salespeople, as a company and cultural imperative, had a workstation where they wrote notes to their customers. It wasn't a "maybe we'll do it" or "if we get a chance later, we'll do a few." It was a complete commitment to the process of customer development, and it resulted in a huge amount of business coming back through their door.

Nathan Jamail wrote in *The Sales Professionals Playbook*, "The more focused you are and the more effort you put into these requirements, the more successful you will be. So embrace it because prospecting is 90 percent discipline and 10 percent skill set and 100 percent necessary."

There are so many vehicles today to help us to clientele better. The delivery vehicles can be handwritten notes, texts, emails, or Facebook messages, but we must communicate appreciation to our customers if we expect them to come back to us. Sending a thank-you message will separate you from the majority of salespeople. Like my friends in San

Diego, I would recommend that you plan your day to allow for thank-you messages, as formalizing the process will help to ensure that you don't overlook this hugely important aspect of sales. Thanking customers for their business is not just the right thing to do; it is also the best way to plant the seeds of future business.

Michelle Stichter, a seasoned retail manager, shared the following story with me.

I took over a store early one year that was struggling to make its numbers and with questionable sales talent—funny how those two so often go hand in hand! One of the first things I did was to require all of my salespeople to complete a client sheet on every guest that visited the store, whether they bought something or not. I coached the team on the kind of language I wanted them to use, statements such as "Allow me to be your personal shopper so that I can let you know if there are any changes with the price or status of this piece."

I had to get the team into the habit of collecting the data, and I would meet with them on a weekly basis to review their client sheets and to give them feedback and encouragement. We would discuss the type of information they were capturing and how it might be used. We also discussed follow-ups, such as thanking the guest for coming into our store, reminding them we were delighted to serve as their personal shopper, or encouraging them to visit us to get their jewelry checked and cleaned. Regular meetings were key to getting the team to embrace the initiative also held them accountable.

Fast-forward a few months, and we found ourselves $32,000 behind plan—thanks in no small part to a few poorly timed snowstorms. On December 23, I gathered the team together and challenged them to hit the clienteling hard. We invited our guests to come in to visit the pieces they had previously viewed and/or we invited them to come in to the post-Christmas sale, scheduled to begin on December 26.

The phone campaign began at eight a.m. on December 26, and in two days, we pulled in $42,000 in sales, easily covering our shortfall. There was a great sense of accomplishment on our team. We had pulled ourselves out of a tough situation because of all of the work we had done with our client-development initiatives. We would never have gotten there without the client sheets. Our efforts produced results, and we could not have been more proud.

As Michelle and her team demonstrated so effectively, realizing results from client-development initiatives requires that you get in the habit of capturing customer information and staying connected to them as appropriate. That means sending thank-you notes (emails and texts can work too, if you sense that the customer would prefer that method) and touching base as appropriate. In an environment where we are subjected to mountains of spam solicitations, both in the mail and digitally, there is something incredibly gratifying about getting a note from a salesperson just to say thanks. I can only imagine how nice that would be.

Setting Goals

"Impossible is a word to be found only in the dictionary
of fools."

—NAPOLEON BONAPARTE

Recently I had the privilege of standing on Commonwealth Avenue to watch the Boston Marathon. As I stood there, caught up in the emotion of the whole spectacle, I saw all kinds of people—older, younger, able-bodied, sight-impaired, amputees, etc. Some of the runners appeared to have been well-prepared, with shoes and clothing that looked like it had been designed for a marathon, while others passed by wearing shoes that looked like they were never intended to sustain 26.2 miles and clothing that was clearly not designed by NASA.

At one point, an older woman ran past me, and as I traced her deliberate and understandably labored steps, I felt humbled, really humbled, at what she was accomplishing. Right as she passed me, she spotted a man in the crowd I later learned was her husband, and she moved over to the side of the road to the barrier behind which he was standing. We were probably standing at the 22- or 23-mile mark, and she was clearly exhausted from her efforts. She reached over the barrier for her husband, and they locked in an embrace for a minute or so.

Watching his obvious pride was something to behold, and he was visibly thrilled at his wife's courage. He seemed to be almost holding her up as they embraced for those precious moments. I managed to snap a couple of pictures with my phone, and when she and her husband said their good-byes and she continued on her run, I approached him to ask if he would like me to send him the pictures.

He was bordering on tears at the emotion of their moment and his wife's accomplishment, and he thanked me for my offer and gave me his email. He then told me that his wife was seventy-one years old, before he boarded the Green Line Trolley that would take him to the finish line and their reunion. Naturally, I would never have asked him how old his wife was, but his volunteering her age seemed to give voice to what I was feeling as I stood there watching her. He too was in awe at what she was doing.

That woman was seventy-one years old and she ran the Boston Marathon. Not being seventy-one, and never having run a marathon, I can't even comprehend what she must have endured to make that happen. I don't know if it was her first or fiftieth race, but here's what I do know: she didn't wake up on April 18, 2016, and decide to transport herself to Hopkinton, Massachusetts, for the purpose of running 26.2 miles into Boston.

She had to have a plan that required countless hours of preparation and hundreds of hours of running through the streets of whatever city she called home. She had to have started with very short distances and built up the miles, as she progressed through the long winter months and into the early days of spring, all with the goal of competing in, and completing, the Boston Marathon. That goal had to have required many sacrifices, and she must invariably have declined numerous opportunities to do other things with friends and family as she pursued her goal. She must have passed on many favorite foods, and possibly preferred beverages, to best prepare herself for the grueling task ahead. Seeing her was an amazing testament to the human spirit, and, as I stood there watching, my decidedly overweight self was none too proud of myself for not yet making my own personal fitness a priority.

As Geoff Colvin wrote in *Talent Is Overrated*:

The best performers judge themselves against a standard that's relevant for what they're trying to achieve. Sometimes they compare their performance with their own personal best; sometimes they compare with the performance of competitors they're facing or expect to face; sometimes they compare with the best-known performance of anyone in the field.

There are two kinds of goals in sales. The most obvious goals are those established by the sales manager. These tend to be very tangible and, one would hope, very realistic; built from a rational place with a real opportunity to make them happen.

The second set of goals are those you set for yourself; and those might include sales goals, personal goals, service goals, customer touches, education goals, etc. These can be both professional and personal goals.

Goal setting is as fundamental to exceptional sales performance as showing up for work. Quite simply, I have never met a successful sales professional who was not ever-cognizant of his or her own goals, and who was not forever striving to meet and beat the next marker. What I also know about outstanding sales performers is that they tend to break their goals down into digestible bites. Just like the woman running that marathon, they make each exercise, each day, each learning opportunity, and each customer contact count. Of course they are aware of what the monthly, quarterly, and annual goals are, but they tend to focus their efforts on specific daily, and sometimes even hourly, actions designed to produce results and keep them on track.

I've met a few people during my career who were not fans of goal-setting. One in particular once suggested that the very idea was absurd, as it suggested, absent the goal, that he would not work as hard or sell as much. While I could understand his logic on some level, I happen not to share his view. Even outstanding performers can stretch and drive themselves beyond their already high standards when they find themselves tracking below their target goals.

My wife was mentoring a business client last week, and she shared with me that the company does not set sales goals. They've got lots of smart people, and they've been around for many years, but goal-setting has just not been their thing. I suspect that particular business is not alone in choosing to not set goals for their business, but their decision not to do so, while confounding on so many levels, should not impact what their best salespeople do. Even in situations like that, you will find that the best salespeople have a plan. They have a sense for what they need to accomplish in a given day, and they very often measure themselves against their own past performance, or a target they have set for themselves.

If you work for a company that does not set goals, set them for yourself. Challenge yourself to meet or exceed certain targets on a day-in and day-out basis. Those targets should be sales results, but they should also be other important goals, such as customer emails, texts, calls, or other contacts. They should include investing a set amount of time each day to embrace new learning opportunities by reading books, blogs, and online publications; listening to podcasts or audiobooks; or watching select TED Talks or YouTube video presentations. Breaking your goals into small, easily digestible bites is the best way to measure your progress on the key performance indicators you want to drive. It's also an excellent way to give yourself regular pats on the back for accomplishing those goals, which, I think we can all agree, isn't such a bad habit to develop.

Rejection and Failure

"Failure is the condiment that gives success its flavor."

—Truman Capote

The old maxim that there are only two certainties in life—death and taxes—ought to be revised to add the following: if you are attempting to make a living in sales, it is 100 percent certain that you will experience failure and rejection every single day. It will visit you in the morning, in the evening, and everywhere in between. You will experience failure and rejection after success, and you will experience failure after failure. It is impossible to exact a healthy living from sales without experiencing failure and rejection on an ongoing basis.

To be clear, my definition of failure and rejection in sales is going to the plate with the bat in your hands and failing to get a hit or a walk, and some days—it happens folks—getting hit by a pitch. In short, you don't even make it to first base, and you very quickly find yourself licking your wounds and spitting sunflower seeds, wondering what the heck happened. How you deal with that ongoing failure goes a long way toward deciding what kind of salesperson you will be. If you have difficulty handling failure and rejection, you are going to have a hard time being successful in sales. To be clear, that doesn't mean that you *like* failure, but it does mean that you accept it as part of the job and you seek to learn from it and use it to help drive your development as a sales professional.

Sales is, on some levels, a math game. Unless you are some kind of freak of nature, you will not be successful closing every prospect. In fact, not only will you not close every prospect, or even most prospects, you will fail more often than you will succeed. The very best salespeople strike out more times than they get a hit. Their conversion rate might be 25 percent or even as high as 40 percent if they are really good, but they will experience considerable rejection and disappointment, and they have to possess the psychological makeup to handle that.

Top salespeople recognize the inevitability of not being able to sell everyone. They understand that even on their best day, their most effective presentation might still result in a customer walking. I can think of many situations during my career when I thought I had hit the ball out of the park, only to come up empty at the end of the day. In fact, as I write this I've been flying across the country, having spent a couple of days calling on customers, and despite feeling generally good about some of the meetings, I am reliving the one that got away, certain that I could have done a much better job to drive a different result.

The best salespeople do not like rejection or failure any more than mediocre salespeople. They can be hard on themselves when things don't go well for them, but they differ from their less successful colleagues in two important ways. For one thing, they are committed to asking for the sale, and they know that because of this they are going to experience lots of rejection. In fact, they understand that the more times they ask for the sale, the more rejection they will encounter.

The second thing is, they differ in how they deal with that rejection. They do not see the customer's no as a rejection of them personally. They may analyze the reasons why the sale wasn't made, they may regret a missed opportunity to have dealt with an obstacle better, and they may second-guess their choices, their timing, even their energy. What they will not do, however, is allow the rejection to define them personally.

I have worked with some superb salespeople in my time, and one of the things I have been most in awe of is how they move on from failure and rejection, with no lack of optimism about the next customer, the next opportunity. Their failure to make a sale is never viewed as a rejection of them personally, and they never allow setbacks to deplete their reserves of energy and enthusiasm. You've often heard the expression, "Like water off a duck's back!" This expression perfectly captures the spirit and the perseverance of great sales drivers.

Weak salespeople, on the other hand, default to clerking sales, a peculiar form of behavior that means they almost wait for the customer to point to the item in question and offer to pay for it. Or, more typically, they continue to engage the customer in inane conversation about anything and everything and dance the shuffle of the reluctant as they hit a brick wall, unable or unwilling to ask for the sale and trapped in a standoff that generally goes nowhere.

Sometimes they escape the uncomfortable deadlock by telling the customer to leave. It can sound like this, "Why don't I write that information down for you, and you can think about it and let me know." Of course, what the salesperson is really saying in that instance is, "Geez, I'm lost here . . . How the heck do I get out of this situation? I can't think of any more stuff to say." What the customer hears in that situation is, "Look, I can't help you. I've thought of everything I can, but I just don't know what you are looking for, and I don't have the skills to figure that out. Why don't you try some other store?"

For the sales clerk, avoiding a direct ask eliminates the possibility of rejection, as you've never actually asked the customer to make a commitment. They don't have to deal with the disappointment of having failed. You can never underestimate what a huge factor rejection-avoidance is in sales. Salespeople without good resilience don't even know that they're doing it, but their need to be okay, to not hear the customer say no, is very real. It often sends them into hiding as they seek any and all distractions, diversions, and tasks to avoid engaging customers, perfectly content to allow other people to engage the customer.

Where this behavior tends to manifest most frequently is in the disparity between how a salesperson with seemingly great people skills can look so effective in executing routine tasks with a customer, yet be so consistently underwhelming in meeting sales goals.

Leonard Mlodinow wrote in *Subliminal: How Your Unconscious Mind Rules Your Behavior*, "The connection between social pain and physical pain illustrates the links between our emotions and the physiological processes of the body. Social rejection doesn't just cause emotional pain; it affects our physical being."

Understanding the impact that rejection can have on salespeople with low resilience, both psychologically and physically, is very important. Their avoidance of situations they feel will reflect poorly on them is quite profound. If you find yourself frequently avoiding the tough questions ("Looks like we've found the perfect gift here. How would you like to pay for that?") or—and this is far more ubiquitous than you might imagine—avoiding customers altogether, it would be worth exploring with trusted friends and/or mentors whether you are really trying to protect yourself from getting hurt.

You have to ask the tough questions as a salesperson, and you need to be able to deal with the inevitable and ongoing rejection that comes with the territory. Rejection is not an indictment of you personally, and you should never allow yourself to be defined by it. You must put into perspective the ratio of sale to no-sale customer interactions and learn to put the misses behind you as quickly as possible. That doesn't mean we can't learn from the no-sale interactions. We should always self-examine and ask ourselves how we might have done better, but we cannot take the rejection so personally that it lessens our energy and expectation for the next customer and the next sale.

The Salesperson-to-Manager Conundrum

> "You can't just excel at sales to be a good manager. Yet, that's precisely how most companies select new front-line managers."

> —FRANK CESPEDES

There are a couple of reasons for the blurred lines one often sees in retail between salespeople and store managers. Retail stores are oftentimes too small to have the luxury of devoting a person 100 percent to "managing." Another reason for the less-than-clear distinction between the two is that many business owners promote their top salespeople into manager positions and, in the process, lose a super salesperson and gain an ineffective manager.

Furthermore, the salesperson who becomes the manager often creates mayhem for the team, as he or she brings an entirely different perspective to managing than is necessary or healthy. A good analogy for this predicament can be found in professional sports, where we sometimes see a former star athlete named as manager. The athlete thinks the management thing is going to be a piece of cake; all the team has to do is to emulate what he used to do when he was a star player. Got it! Ah, I think not.

Managing people is a decidedly more complex challenge, and it requires, among many other skills, subverting your own ego so that you can manage salespeople at their own unique level—each different from the other—and really listen to people, even when your instinct might be to run for the hills or, for that matter, to send the salesperson in question out to pasture. Asking a top salesperson who has just assumed the role of manager to subvert their ego is, as someone once said, a little like putting a Post-it on the ocean.

This salesperson-to-manager cycle tends to rinse and repeat over and over again, and presents a real predicament for store owners. Top salespeople become top salespeople in the first place because of their strong ego-drive. It is, ironically, that very ego-drive that feeds their aspiration to become managers, even as the specific job requirements of actually *managing* prove to be a far cry from what excites and interests top salespeople.

So why does it happen so much? The title and the requisite responsibility are often perceived as a promotion (with greater recognition, reward, responsibility, compensation, etc.) when, in fact, it can be anything but, as it dumps a whole host of not-very-interesting responsibilities onto someone who was previously very successful at managing him or herself to outstanding performance. These salespeople were able to focus their efforts on their own performance, and they did not have to manage colleagues, many of them less skilled than they, to better performance. In assuming the manager position, they effectively move from a place where they were able to be very selective in how and where they devoted their time and energy to a situation where they are sometimes consumed by the most mundane of responsibilities.

Unless your definition of a manager is really just a great salesperson with a set of keys, you are, all of a sudden, asking a top salesperson to be an effective administrator, a personnel manager, a customer-service champion, a coach, an organizer of schedules and training, a motivator of people, some of whom he or she might not have given a minute's thought to previously, a good interviewer, and, occasionally, the bearer of bad news, as the unsavory task of firing people needs to be handled with sensitivity and care.

The skill set necessary to be a great manager is very different than that required to be a top salesperson. If business owners and managers recognize great sales talent for what it is (the very lifeblood of the business), they ought to be able to construct great opportunities for the top salespeople to use their talents in challenging and engaging ways, instead of making them managers. It is not a favor to anyone when a great salesperson becomes a poor manager.

The "promotion" happens because the owner values the performance of the salesperson, and he or she does not want to risk losing them by "denying" them the opportunity to advance their career. So, if we are not going to turn our top performers into managers, what do we do with them? Must we risk losing them as they likely seek that recognition elsewhere?

Top salespeople should be recognized and challenged in ways that reward their wiring and accomplishments. That starts by making sure they are paid commensurate with their contributions to the business. I have personally been in management situations where the top salespeople were making more money than me, and that is how it should be. Any perspective in a business that sees top salespeople as down the pecking order, below the manager, is misguided.

Some examples of how you might engage top salespeople include using them for select training opportunities, bringing them to trade shows, and including them in the buying (influencing) process. They can be included in important conversations that concern developments in the store, including matters of hiring. Sending them to industry conferences, educational events, seminars, and other learning opportunities for their professional and personal development should also be considered. They have a right to expect professional development, and the business owner has an obligation to make that happen.

If you read this chapter as a business owner or manager and your only takeaway is that you should *not* make your top salespeople into managers, then you are leaving out the hugely important flip side of that coin. You *can't do nothing* and expect your best salespeople to be satisfied in a company that makes no investment in them. To do so is to invite them to look elsewhere, and you will either lose them completely or ensure that they become disengaged, an equally tragic loss.

To be fair, some salespeople do go on to become very good managers. They tend not to be the very top sales performers, and evidence of their management capabilities would likely have been visible in their day-to-day performance; as they organized the team, volunteered their time to develop initiatives, attended trainings, and worked with their colleagues to help them overcome challenges. They may also have shown a discipline and organization not always present with the best salespeople.

If you decide to promote a salesperson who meets the aforementioned criteria, you will be doing it because the job aligns with their wiring, not because they have the biggest ego on the team, and you feel like you have to do it for defensive reasons. We'll look at the task of managing salespeople in the next few chapters. This should be of interest to managers and, I hope, salespeople who may aspire to that role, or to those who think they want it, but who might recalibrate their aspiration with a better understanding of what the position ought to look like.

Managing Salespeople

Managing Salespeople

"It was the best of times, it was the worst of times."

—CHARLES DICKENS

Managing salespeople has never been an easy undertaking for any number of reasons. It might be the combination of a very good manager and a not-so-good team. It might be a very good team and a not-so-good manager. Perhaps you have a good team *and* a good manager, but they are both denied the resources to do great work by the owner of the business. In that situation, invoke the first rule of holes—when you find yourself in one, stop digging and find somewhere else to work.

Since this chapter is called Managing Salespeople, I won't speak to the insanely important job of actually hiring the right talent in the first place. If you are typically tasked with that responsibility, please refer to my book *Hiring Squirrels* for some helpful pointers in that area. If your responsibilities include building compensation plans, you might find the chapter on Meritocracy helpful.

Salespeople don't work for companies, organizations, or stores. They work for people—and there is no more important person in a store than the manager. The manager has an opportunity to engage, inspire, and influence the performance and professional quality-of-life for his salespeople. That doesn't mean that he can turn a bad salesperson into a good one, but he can manage to effect the best return on the talents at his disposal. That said, while a good manager cannot turn a weak salesperson into a good one if that person does not have the necessary wiring (drive, empathy, and resilience), he or she can absolutely destroy a good salesperson.

Keith Rosen wrote in *Coaching Salespeople into Champions*:

> What do people want most in their careers? Statistics show that people want the positive reinforcement and acknowledgement that lets them know they are doing a good job. The number-one issue people have in the workforce today is "Will I be valued and will I have a job in the future?" You want the people who are working for you to want to be there. Otherwise, what do you think they are going to spend their time doing?

Engaged employees will always perform at a higher level than those who are just going through the motions, because they are not entirely committed, either to the job or to the company. It might also be because they don't have the necessary wiring to do the job well and, as such, they feel like a square peg in a round hole. Possibly they have actively disengaged, a consequence of weak management or, at least, the perception of weak management.

No matter what the circumstances, an employee who is not engaged is a tremendous loss for a business, especially when that salesperson has otherwise been a solid producer. The lost revenues and customer opportunities can be lethal to a business that needs every sale and every customer it can get.

Alternately, weaker sales performers may also be disengaged, and they can be a particularly huge drain on the business, as they do *just enough* to not call unwanted attention (performance scrutiny) to themselves and still don't produce results or contribute to the overall customer experience.

A manager has a great responsibility and a great opportunity to mold a winning formula. The atmosphere, environment, and culture is, in many respects, a function of who the manager is, what she does, and how she manages her team. Even in situations where the manager is denied key resources to do her job, she can still create the conditions for success by rallying her team around the goals and aspirations of the business and by playing up the *we're a winning team* ethos. There can be an element of "To heck with them (owners, corporate etc.). Let's show them that we can do this in spite of them, so let's be successful for each other and make the best of this situation."

The flip side of that coin, however, is that the manager can be the single biggest problem on a team and can, by design or default, create an environment that is almost antithetical to success. Keith Rosen wrote in *Coaching Salespeople into Sales Champions*, "The atmosphere, tone, and culture created within a company lead back to the efforts, actions, and behavior of one person—the manager."

The qualities that are essential to being a great manager—willingness to listen and subvert one's own ego, strong communication skills, the courage to be respectfully direct when necessary, and to manage the very best from a disparate group of individuals who cannot, by definition, all be managed the same way—are not necessarily conducive to people who have previously been star sales performers.

As mentioned earlier, a manager must be willing to appeal to the best talents of each of her people, recognizing as she must that one of the paradoxes of great team performance is the ability and willingness to manage individuals as individuals. They cannot be all managed the same way. Each employee has his or her own hot buttons. Some need a quiet word, others a more assertive and direct communication. Some employees want to be left to work through their challenges alone, and others need a more hands-on approach.

Top sales producers don't typically subvert their ego as a rule, and yet managing in a sales environment demands that the manager has the drive and ambition of a top sales performer but the emotional maturity to understand that it requires all kinds of people to make a team work. A team cannot be stacked with superstar performers, and it cannot be entirely populated with really pleasant and easy to manage midlevel and low-level performers.

One of the most important aspects of managing teams is establishing a common purpose. You just can't have people showing up every day and going through the motions. They must have something to believe in and a clear understanding of what is expected of them. There's no doubt that understanding the business objectives and sales goals of the store are hugely important; we are in the business of selling stuff, a fact that is all too often lost on weak managers, who believe that managing schedules, doing paperwork, and handling customer service issues is their sole purpose for existing. But beyond meeting sales targets, there has to be a higher purpose, something for the team to believe in, and something to pick people up when things are not going so well.

The need for employees to be engaged in their work, in their purpose, was never more profoundly articulated than when Brian Brim wrote in *The Best of the Gallup Management Journal 2001—2007*:

Through analysis of its database of 1.4 million employees in 66 countries, Gallup researchers have identified an inverse relationship between employee engagement, or the degree to which a worker is fulfilled by his or her job, and length of service, or number of years he or she has been with the company. That means that, for most employees, the first year on the job is their best. It's downhill from there for the worker and for the company as well, because disengaged employees are a drag on profit, sales, and overall satisfaction among customers.

Engaging employees is not something that is accomplished during a new-hire orientation. You can't simply check a box and expect that the employee will be good thereafter. Engaging people is a function of consistency in language and behavior, executed daily in decisions large and small, and built around a common purpose. Gallup's research has shown that 50 percent of workers are not engaged at work and 20 percent are actively disengaged, a very damaging and insidious place to be and something, if we are being honest, that ought to be a major priority for a good manager.

The manager must create a trusting environment and a consistent standard of behavior for the store and business, and yet she must respect the reality that salespeople cannot all be managed the same way. She has to be able to be a chameleon and adopt whatever positions will illicit the best performance from a given employee. Hiding behind claims of being fair and equitable in order to not manage people as individuals is just plain naive.

A counterintuitive, if not paradoxical, principle is that is good managers spend more time with their best people, not their stragglers. As Marcus Buckingham and Curt Coffman wrote in their brilliant book, *First, Break All the Rules*, "great managers invest in their best because it is extremely productive to do so and actively destructive to do otherwise." Excepting that there are always going to be disparities between those salespeople who have the inherent wiring for sales and those who do not, spending more time with those people who are the most productive is simply better business.

Don't Be That Guy

"Generally, he is insane, but every once in a while he has
lucid moments where he is just plain stupid."

—Anonymous

I'm not sure that there is anything more irritating or ineffective than a weak manager. And, quite honestly, I don't feel the need to spell out all of the ways a manager can be weak. It doesn't matter how great the company is, how wonderful the compensation plan, or how decent the owner of the business is. If you install (and support) a crap manager and allow him to infect and infest your organization, your best people will go someplace else.

One of the common traits of ineffective managers is the delusion that they need to know everything, to have all the answers. This competence delusion, beyond what is real or reasonable, is a very slippery slope that sends all the wrong signals to your team. In the first instance, it suggests that you are somehow always the smartest guy in the room. In the second instance, it paints you as a bit of an ego maniac, without the humility to admit that you might occasionally be wrong, or that anyone else could ever illuminate a discussion on important matters.

Asking for help from your team demonstrates that you are open and honest and that you do value their feedback. It communicates that building a team matters to you and that you are not arrogant enough to dismiss the contributions from your team, that you do value and respect their input. Stubborn insistence on going solo, when faced with important decisions, might be one of the great paradoxes of management. The desire to come up with all of the answers alone, deluding yourself in the belief that doing so reflects positively on your capabilities, actually sends the opposite message. It suggests a lack of emotional maturity, and that you lack the humility, the empathy, and the authenticity to do the right thing for the business and for your people. It takes all kinds of people to make up a team, and it is, quite frankly, ridiculous to believe that even on the most challenged teams there is not great feedback to be had on any given topic.

Adam Grant wrote in *Give and Take*:

Research shows that at work, the vast majority of giving that occurs between people is in response to direct requests for help. In one study, managers described times when they gave and received help. Of all the giving exchanges that occurred, roughly 90 percent were initiated by the recipient asking for help. Much of the time, we're embarrassed: we don't want to look incompetent or needy, and we don't want to burden others.

As Grant suggests, of course, far from looking needy or incompetent, there is great strength in reaching out to the team for help. It shows them that you respect their opinions and that you are interested in their point of view on matters that generally involve them anyway. In many respects, it is the highest form of respect, provided, of course, it is done in an authentic way and that you really do listen to the feedback. It does not mean that you will always agree with or chart the course that is preferable to the team, but if you listen with respect and sincere interest to their feedback, and then explain why you need to take a given course of action, you will be far more likely to have the team's buy-in than if you had acted in an autocratic manner and excluded them altogether.

Whenever you are putting together a meeting to discuss an important matter, never start by stating your point of view and always encourage respectful debate, even to the point of having someone play the devil's advocate. Another idea is to have each of the members of the teams write out their thoughts in advance of a meeting so that all points of view are considered without bias and without intimidation, intended or otherwise. You are not being open or fair if you open the meeting by forcefully articulating what you would like to happen.

Managing Baggage

"People are not your most important asset. The right
people are."

—JIM COLLINS

It is much easier to build a team of salespeople who get along well with each other than it is to build a team who will be successful in accomplishing goals and driving the business forward, despite some tensions among the players. Mark de Rond wrote in *There Is an I in Team*, "A healthy level of internal competition can help get the best out of high performers. To try to suppress any competitive elements may do the team a great disservice." That is, of course, unless your real objective is to have a happy crew and you are willing to trade that harmony for lost business.

Look, great salespeople come with baggage. It's as simple as that. I wrote about it in an earlier chapter, and I am repeating it here because it's something you need to contend with if you want to be a successful manager. I am not recommending that you seek out people with baggage, but if you don't have some baggage to manage on your team, you probably don't have real sales drivers.

Top sales performers might have a predilection to tardiness, a habit of being untidy, they may profile customers beyond your comfort level, and they might be short and dismissive of their colleagues on occasions.

Their baggage could be any combination of these traits, and the combination of great salespeople and baggage is as predictable as summer and ice cream.

De Rond wrote, "High performers are unusually restless. As a recent survey of one hundred high achievers suggests, their single most common trait was discontent. Restlessness fuels productivity. But it can cause people to be impatient with those around them as well."

There are any number of reasons they might be hard to manage, and, quite frankly, with few exceptions, you need to figure a way to deal with it. That doesn't mean that you give up trying to get the top performers to conform to a reasonable standard of accommodation in areas they might otherwise be falling down in, but you should try and maintain a healthy perspective that the wiring of focused (on customers, on sales) salespeople, and their unrelenting drive for top billing, is one of the hardest talents to uncover and ought to be managed as such.

One way to manage baggage is to maintain an ongoing dialogue, built upon a platform of mutual respect, with your top salespeople. That can be as simple as requiring them to make a sincere effort to mitigate identified shortcomings in exchange for some leeway on your part. In the jewelry business, for instance, that might mean that you will give up asking them to become display aficionados if they agree to leave the display cases in some sense of order after they have been in them. You might look for opportunities here and there to turn a blind eye to minor shortcomings or infractions and cover for them every now and again. Some of you may find that idea offensive and unfair; different standards for different salespeople and all that jazz. Here's the deal: get over it.

Great salespeople are already on a different level than their less successful colleagues, and they have earned the right to be cut some slack every now and again. That's the way the world works, and if you don't believe me, look around you. Are the best athletes treated the same as the guys filling out the roster? Is that lead singer going to be managed the same way as a backup singer? Is George Clooney treated the same way as an extra on the set? Great salespeople are a very precious commodity, and it is a big mistake to attempt to treat them the same way you would your non-performers. They are more passionate, more driven, harder on themselves, more likely to be there for you when the going gets tough. When you need some added firepower because you've had a bad sales day, week, or month, where do you go for help?

Embrace baggage, but know too that a salesperson who is toxic, and I mean really toxic, needs to be gone at the earliest opportunity. No matter how effective a person is in driving sales, if he or she demonstrates consistently unethical behavior, and demonstrates a blatant disregard for the basic conventions of decency and respect, they should be invited to find another job. There is a very big difference between a salesperson with baggage and a salesperson who has serious character issues that threaten the very culture of the business and negatively impact your employees and customers.

These traits might be as bad as outright theft, disguised as aggressive sales habits, consistent bullying of team members, or flagrant disregard and outright disrespect of the manager and/or owner of the business. Note that I am not talking about a passionate, even heated, exchange of views on a sensitive matter, but a pattern of undermining behavior, over an extended period time.

One very important note of caution is that a top salesperson may become frustrated with what he or she perceives as a bad manager. I accept that it is very difficult to be objective about your own performance, but before you allow yourself to place the *toxic* label on an otherwise top performer, ask yourself if you might be the problem. Far too many weak managers readily apply *toxic* or similar monikers to top salespeople, when what they are really saying is that they do not have the will or the capacity, intellectually and/or emotionally, to manage them.

Remember, you should not be looking to build an *easy-to-manage* team where everyone gets along at the cost of driving business. What you need is a dynamic team of complimentary and occasionally contentious members that can ensure a healthy level of competitive tension. Harmony is awfully good in music, but it rarely plays well in the fiercely competitive world of retail sales.

Develop Relationships

"The desire for social approval is a fundamental human motivation."

—Jonah Berger

Many moons ago, when I was fresh off the boat, so to speak, I had a manager named Leonard. He was a control freak, and he felt that it was his role to remain aloof from the team, separate and unequal. He never let his guard down, he seemed to be in a state of perpetual anxiety, and he made no effort to engage with his "underlings" in any way, shape, or form. He would tell people what hours they were working (no discussion there), he would publicly admonish employees for mistakes he witnessed or perceived, and he would sell in a style that might best be described on a continuum somewhere between manic and panic. Without a modicum of hesitation, I will tell you that Leonard was a freakin' disaster as a manager.

No one on our team really knew who Leonard was, and not one of us would ever volunteer, metaphorically speaking, to lay down on the tracks for him. He was, in many respects, the poster child for a crappy manager. I think about Leonard from time to time, and I wonder what ever became of him, and whether he is enjoying a fulfilling life and career. I wonder whether any of his ex-employees ever kept in touch with him after they had gone their separate ways, and whether any of them would call him a friend.

Leonard made no effort to engage his team. He didn't want to know what anyone did outside of work, he never asked about our families or friends, or whether we had any interesting hobbies or activities. We could only have speculated about the kind of person he was outside of work because he never invited anyone to a social event or dinner, or volunteered any information about himself.

Robin Sharma, in *The Leader Who Had No Title*, wrote, "You spend the best hours of the best days of the best years of your life among those you work with. Doesn't it make sense to really get to know them and have superb relationships with them? You'll make friends. You'll feel a sense of belonging. You'll have a feeling of an encouraging community all around you."

Great managers open themselves up to their people. They engage with their teams in a way that is transparent and authentic. They are not only unafraid to enjoy social time and activities with their team, but they actively seek them out. They create an environment in their place of business that is friendly, supportive, and professional. They can have a beer with their subordinates and still have their respect when they have to have a difficult conversation the next day. Participating with the team in a karaoke night or joining a softball league together is a great bonding experience.

We had a tradition at one of the Tiffany stores I worked for of all gathering to sing Christmas carols before we opened the door on Christmas Eve. It was by the employees and for the employees, and it was a special bonding experience shared by everyone—managers, salespeople, and the operations team. When I left that store to move to another part of the country, I received a gift from that team that remains to this day one of the most wonderful gifts I have ever received. It was a beautiful photograph album, and it contained a photo of each employee. Each member of the team had then taken the time to write a personal note next to their photograph.

Trust Your People

"People generally see what they look for, and hear what they listen for."

—HARPER LEE

If you cannot trust as a *default position*, you really have no business managing people. Trust is the essential foundation of any relationship, and I take issue with the idea that it has to be "earned." In my worldview, I will trust you until your actions and behavior demonstrate, without a shadow of a doubt, that you should lose that trust. If that happens, our relationship will exist on an entirely different level, if at all. Depending on the infraction, I might give you the opportunity to rebuild the trust.

Derlega, Winstead, and Jones wrote in *Personality, Contemporary Theory and Research*:

> The tendency to trust others is not only essential for social inter-
> actions and social structure but also has been found to be related
> to constructive problem solving, effective strategies for seeking
> social and emotional support, better health, and more effective
> coping under stress. People higher in trust also have been found
> to be happier and better adjusted whereas, by contrast, low trust
> has been linked to emotional distress and anxiety.

You simply cannot approach a professional relationship with the view that someone might not perform, or might let you down. Once you have made the hiring decision, or assumed the role of managing an existing team, you are much more likely to win the trust of the team (without which you will not be an effective manager) if you give each person your complete trust. Micromanaging, looking over employees' shoulders, and concerning yourself with what people might be saying about you or the company is a needless waste of energy, and it will drive you and/or your team into a state of paranoia and dysfunction.

If you find yourself in a situation where you are having difficulty trusting people on your team, one of two things is certain: you have either hired the wrong people—in which case you ought to review your hiring practices—or *you* might be in the wrong job. I repeat, you cannot be a good manager of people if you are inherently mistrusting of them. If the latter is true, there might be a home-based job or a cubicle someplace waiting for your unique talents, but you should probably *not* be managing people.

We all need to feel some control and ownership in our work environment. No matter what the job, we need to believe that it is ours to do, and that we have the trust of the people we work for. That is a fundamental human need, and it is evident even in infants.

Many years ago, I was interviewing with someone who would ultimately become a great influence in my career. As the interview progressed, he sensed that I might not have been as excited about the prospect of working for his company as he was in hiring me. He paused for just a moment and then, looking straight at me, asked, "What is your biggest fear as you think about this job?"

It was a great way to get me to take ownership in the conversation. My response to him was, "Accountability without empowerment."

I wanted to be given the rope, to be trusted to do the job, to be given the tools and the resources to move the bar. I have often thought about that question and my response in the years since, and I believe that both have stood the test of time. My response to his great question was deeply rooted in a desire that we all have to feel like we are in control of our work. We need to be trusted, and we need some measure of control over our working environment.

Dan Gilbert wrote in *Stumbling on Happiness*, "Human beings come into the world with a passion for control, they go out of the world the same way, and research suggests that if they lose their ability to control things at any point between their entrance and their exit, they become unhappy, helpless, hopeless, and depressed."

You cannot create a trusting environment and workplace without giving people some control over their work. That can take many forms, including how their work or day is structured, giving them control over the music that is played, when they take lunch, giving some leeway for a mental break now and again, etc. Attempting to micromanage an employee's every waking (working) moment is just poor management and rooted in mistrust.

Now, I unapologetically confess that there is a certain paradox in saying that there are two separate standards for trust. For employees, it must be given at employment and continued throughout the manager/ employee relationship unless you are given a compelling reason to withdraw that trust. However, for the manager, trust must be earned over a longer period of time as a consequence of his or her consistency of words, actions, and behaviors with each individual team member, and with the group as a whole.

Robert Levin and Joseph Rosse write in *Talent Flow*, "Trust develops slowly over months and years of actions—but it can be destroyed in a moment with a serious violation of what work psychologists refer to as a psychological contract, the often-unstated but very real expectations that employees and employers hold about one another."

I took that job that day, and I ended up spending four of the most rewarding years of my career learning from the man who had interviewed me. The environment and culture were far from ideal, but the opportunity to do good work and to exert influence over my own environment was always there.

Quit Being Florence Nightingale

> "Focus on the critical few and not the insignificant
> many."

> —ANONYMOUS

Florence Nightingale was a British nurse who chartered new territory when she led a team of nurses to tend to wounded British soldiers in the war against the Russian Empire in Crimea in 1854. Her courage and bravery in tending to the neediest rightly cemented her place in the history books. To this day, we frequently hear the term "Florence Nightingale complex" when someone takes on a huge cause, sometimes a losing cause, and it is rarely invoked as a positive.

Here's a newsflash: quit being Florence Nightingale in your role as a manager and spend less time with your weaker salespeople! In fact, spend far less time with them. Again, I confess that idea is counterintuitive, and yet I must insist upon challenging the assumption that devoting your efforts to fixing your weaker salespeople is a good investment of a manager's time. I am not referring to orientation time, or the requisite and necessary product, policy, or customer-experience initiatives. I am referring, most explicitly, to efforts designed to turn poor-performing salespeople into top sales performers.

As we have discussed at length, you cannot coach the necessary wiring into a salesperson who does not possess it, and if you honestly assess the reasons you typically spend time with non-performers, if often comes back to poor sales results. And, in more cases than not, these poor sales results are usually chronic. There can be something of a Groundhog Day effect as you find yourself talking about the same things over and over again in an effort to coax a better outcome from underperforming salespeople.

We all have a finite amount of hours for employee development, and spending a majority of that time with your strongest performers is a better strategy if you want to grow your business and continue to get the best from your top performers. Marcus Buckingham and Donald Clifton wrote in *Now, Discover Your Strengths*, "Since the greatest room for each person's growth is in the areas of his strength, you should focus your training time and money on educating him about his strengths and figuring out ways to build on these strengths rather than on remedially trying to plug his 'skills gaps.'"

Any reasonable assessment of time spent managing salespeople would likely reveal that a manager spends more time putting out fires and trying to improve the sales performance of her weaker players. It's as if we convince ourselves that the top performers are doing just fine and that they don't need a lot of our time. We rationalize that because the top players are self-starters and, notwithstanding the baggage that must be managed from time to time, don't cry out for a lot of attention, at least not overtly, that we are okay leaving them to their own devices.

Ironically, therein lies the danger, in terms of what it costs the business in the short term (top performers can become disillusioned if they feel they are being ignored) and also in the longer term, as they often decide to take their talents elsewhere. This is a particularly hard pill to swallow as, unlike the ongoing discussions/coaching and pep talks you might be having with underperformers, the top salespeople can shock the system when they finally tell you they are leaving. The warning signs just didn't seem to be there leading up to that unfortunate and all too often irreversible conversation, because you were just too busy trying to fix the unfixable.

Your best people need to be told that they are doing a good job, and they need your engagement in projects from time to time. They do not need or want to be micromanaged, and they most certainly won't tolerate inauthenticity or being patronized. Ian Robertson wrote in *The Winner Effect*:

> There are many domains of human endeavor where people get enormous satisfaction—a sense of reward which fired up the brain's dopamine systems—from doing a job well, contributing to a cause, or achieving a goal. The respect and admiration of others is an even more potent source of dopamine reward in the brain. The approval of a respected boss can be more intrinsically rewarding for an employee than a financial bonus.

The simple law of mathematics is yet another powerful reason to heed the clarion call of investing in your best people. In short, if your efforts with each employee result in a percentage improvement in performance, where would you prefer to see that percentage increase, with the lower-producing salesperson, or with the higher producers? In most instances, the disparity between the top performers and the non-performers can be significant, and the resulting return on your investment will always reflect that chasm.

Wanting to help weak performers to higher levels of performance is very admirable. It appeals to the Florence Nightingale in all of us, and on those rare occasions when it actually works, it feels pretty darn good. You might even have a little hero dust sprinkled on you from time to time, but it just isn't a good strategy. If you are going to fish for dinner, cast your line where the fish are swimming. The odds are much better that you'll eat supper.

Praise Publicly and Make It Real

"Recognition is a need we all crave, and there are no exceptions."

—ABRAHAM MASLOW

Most mothers, at some point or other, probably cautioned their sons and daughters to say nothing about a person unless it was good. As with most things moms say and do, that generally sound counsel has a solid spine of good sense and serves those smart enough to adhere to it in professional life too. When it comes to managing salespeople, however, it should be taken with a just a pinch of salt.

Your responsibility as a manager requires that you balance your feedback between positive affirmation and constructive criticism. How you position the positive and negative feedback often determines how you will be perceived as a manager by your team. I'll discuss negative feedback in the next chapter, but I need to point out that an equally wet blanket can be thrown over an employee by not praising them in the right way.

Everyone needs to be acknowledged and, as Maslow said, there are no exceptions. The recognition ought to be done publicly and authentically. When I say publicly, that could be in a structured or formal setting such as a sales meeting. However, it could also be a positive word in the moment, in public, to acknowledge something worthwhile. A simple, "Hey, I love the way you handled that situation" can be very effective in communicating to a salesperson that you are paying attention to their good work.

If you notice it, say it. Again, it does not have to be a big deal, and you should not feel compelled to wait for the *perfect time*. Do it when you see it, and mean it. Depending on the subject, it can be a simple comment noting the behavior, or a more formal recognition in a group or team setting.

Good deeds, actions, and accomplishments should be acknowledged across the board. It is, perhaps, an entirely understandable human failing to disproportionately want to praise the less successful members of our team, who, quite frankly, just don't get as many wins as the top performers. And why not? There is great reward in seeing an underperformer make an important sale, or witnessing a worthy breakthrough from someone who has been struggling. Encouraging such success can help build self-confidence, and that is, of course, a very important ingredient in having sales success.

We have, however, a tendency to be a little more frugal in our praise of top performers. We see them enjoy more frequent successes, and there is a real danger in taking that success for granted. Top performers expect the best of themselves. They are motivated self-starters, and they are the first to hold themselves accountable for sales failures. But be warned: they need to hear the manager's feedback just as much as anyone else, or you may see their usually great passion turn inward and become destructive. Far too many top salespeople feel like their efforts are taken for granted, and for too many managers the realization of not having acknowledged their successes can come too late, as we find out that their feeling of not being respected results in them having taken another job.

Alain de Botton wrote in *Status Anxiety*:

There is something at once sobering and absurd in the extent to which we are lifted by the attention of others and sunk by their disregard. Our mood may blacken because a colleague greets us distractedly or our telephone calls go unreturned. And we are capable of thinking life worth living because someone remembers our name or sends us a fruit basket.

But be warned, there is nothing so shallow as false praise or contrived admiration. In those awkward and inauthentic situations, not only does the kudos fail to serve its purpose, but it actually creates a negative experience for both the target of the praise and his or her colleagues. Be specific when you are giving praise and make sure the acknowledgement is appropriate and genuine.

To reiterate, the praise can and should be served while it is hot. When you see someone doing something good, make mention of it at that moment, or at the earliest opportunity thereafter. Do not wait until the moment has passed, unless it cannot be avoided, and again note that praise-worthy behaviors and actions don't have to be groundbreaking. If something happens that captures your attention as being noteworthy, say something. Of course, if the action you are acknowledging is a good teaching moment for other salespeople, return to it at the appropriate time and use it as a good example of how a given situation was handled.

Keith Rosen wrote in *Coaching Salespeople into Sales Champions*, "Why don't we praise our employees enough? Why are we so stingy with our acknowledgement? What are we afraid might happen? Do we feel that we only have a limited supply of acknowledgement and we don't want to use it up?"

Certain managers are going to be more comfortable than others in publicly acknowledging worthy performance. For some, it comes very easily, and for others, it needs to become more of a habit. In the grand scheme of things, however, it simply must be viewed and practiced as an essential part of your job, and is central to your efforts to build a team that respects and responds to you.

One of the great historical sporting accomplishments was Roger Bannister's breaking of the four-minute mile barrier in 1954. On running in front of Finnish athletic fans, Bannister wrote, "They reserve their applause so that they do not debase its currency." I laughed aloud when I read the line in his autobiography, *The Four-Minute Mile*, as I simply could not imagine conveying what he was trying to say in fewer, or any more appropriate, words. So, with a tip of my cap to the great Bannister, let us be reminded that exercising our capacity for applause and recognition is not only admirable, but downright essential. I can assure you, its currency will not be debased.

Criticism Should Be Private, Constructive, and Specific

"He has a right to criticize, who has a heart to help."

—ABRAHAM LINCOLN

The flip side of the praise coin is, of course, having to tell people when their performance has not been up to par. This particular aspect of the job comes easier to some than to others, but it does not have to be the stressor that it can sometimes be if a manager embraces certain disciplines.

First, any criticism must be balanced with a requisite amount of positive feedback as warranted. Any perception that you are piling on, or looking for fault, will go a long way toward diluting whatever the desired result is for giving the feedback in the first place. Unless, of course, you criticize for sport, in which case you are the problem, not the employee.

Second, the criticism should be delivered in private, and it should be very specific. Empty platitudes such as "You've just got to do better" and "I'm not satisfied with your work" are useless at best, and downright demotivating at the worst. Criticism ought to be delivered in a respectful manner and in private, with specificity and detailed, actionable steps. Examples such as "Joe, your sales numbers are off by 20 percent from last month. One of the things I have noticed is that you are waiting on fewer customers than I am used to seeing from you. The foot traffic has been good, so can you help me understand what might be impacting that?"

In the above scenario, you have identified the problem (Joe's sales are off by 20 percent), and you have given him a specific data point (he's just not getting to as many customers as he should) to consider. He may come back to you and tell you that a project you asked him to take on is keeping him off the floor more than he would like, or there may be other very tangible impediments that are keeping him from meeting his numbers. No matter what the reason, having a direct, respectful, and specific conversation will enable you and the employee to work on a solution.

In my experience, few people set out to do bad work. There may be a skills issue if you are asking someone to do something that they are just not capable of doing. There may be an issue that is not evident to you (a strained relationship with a coworker, frustration over a new policy that has delivered unintended consequences, or a feeling that you are perhaps not as supportive as you should be). There might also be an issue outside of work that is having a detrimental effect on the employee (illness, issues or concerns with a family member, financial stresses, etc.). The only way to find out what is going on with the employee's performance is to create a proper environment for a conversation (ideally, free of interruptions and in private) and to enter into that conversation with specifics and an open mind. State your concerns clearly and respectfully, and listen to what the employee has to say. There's a very good chance that you might hear something that will enlighten your understanding of the issues and enable you work with the employee in a supportive manner to get him back on track.

Of course, if the feedback relates to something said or done that was off-brand for your store, a quiet word about why this was not the best thing to have said or done should be all that is needed. As with all constructive criticism, make sure to keep things in perspective. If you are dealing with a salesperson who is generally a very good employee, the last thing you want to do is to overdramatize a matter that can be handled with sensitivity and a word of support.

Christopher Porath and Christine Pearson wrote in their *Harvard Business Review* article "The Price of Incivility":

> Through a poll of 800 managers and employees in 17 industries, we learned just how people's reactions play out. Among workers who've been on the receiving end of incivility, 80% lost work-time worrying about the incident, 78% said that their commitment to the organization declined, 25% admitted to taking their frustrations out on the customers.

There is quite simply never an excuse for disrespect or incivility when you are coaching an employee. Whatever your intent may have been, it will quickly fall by the wayside and any hoped-for acknowledgment or improvement will have been lost in the poor delivery. Be civil, respectful, and supportive, and always agree on a specific course of action to improve performance.

There were some great comments, such as Beverly's: "You made it fun and a great learning experience." Tim's "I thank you for being you and for giving me the opportunity to come to this company . . . for being observant and for looking out for others." "Each life touches so many other lives, and I'm glad you touched mine," James wrote. And finally, from Catherine, who just lost her brave battle with cancer this very week, "You have been such a positive influence in my life and I cannot thank you enough."

My time with that team was a gift to me. It was a gift because I allowed myself to get to know those people. To connect with them in a way that was not judgmental, that had no bias or agenda. It was just a beautiful collection of human beings doing the best they could for each other and for the store we all worked for. We had our stresses and challenges, and life sometimes got in the way as we all dealt with our own ups and downs. We even had death delivered to our doorstep, losing two colleagues during my time there, but the strength and camaraderie of that team helped to pull us through even in those darkest days.

As Robin Sharma wrote:

> View people accurately as they are, but always treat them with such respect and kindness that they quickly step into all that you dreamed they could be. Make the time each day amid the chaos of your everyday tasks to grow your relationships, offer those around you a smile, or a caring gesture.

The best managers are authentic and open. They don't suit up for work and act differently than they would at home; they are transparent, approachable, and engaging. They take the time to get to know their people, and they demonstrate in their words and actions that they care about each member of the team. They can let their guard down and enjoy some self-effacing humor, and they can still be clear, decisive, and direct when having to confront sensitive issues with various team members. They don't pretend to have *all* the answers, and they are not afraid to ask for help when they need it.

No Negativity

"Some people do really find fault like there's a reward
for it."

—Zig Ziglar

One of the most important tasks for a manager is to maintain a positive working environment for the team. That can be an easier undertaking if the group dynamic is strong, and if people enjoy each other's company and generally get along. It is a far more difficult job if some members of the team do not particularly enjoy the company of their colleagues.

As we discussed in an earlier chapter, it is easier to construct a team of people that get along well than it is to put together a team that is productive, despite some tensions on the team. In all likelihood, your team is neither a Kumbaya-style group, where all the members enjoy each other's company, nor is it a tension-filled group, perpetually on the verge of anarchy and revolt.

If your team is a harmonious group, I would guess that you are likely trading a ton of business in exchange for accord. Quite simply, I have never—and I mean never—witnessed a beautifully harmonious team that wasn't doing some sleepwalking through lost business on a regular basis.

You need creative and competitive tension, and if you are a successful business, you will almost certainly have some of both. It comes from the friction that is caused when you put strong performers and non-performers in the same business. Top performers tend to conduct themselves in a way that is energized, focused, and results-oriented, and they rarely slow down for what they consider to be petty obstacles or speed bumps. That aggressiveness can agitate non-performers, who regularly point to rule breaking, or at least rule bending, by the top performers as the *very reason* they are more successful.

The characterization is, of course, absurd. While there is truth to the notion that top performers challenge rules and convention to get results, they do that *because* they are successful; they are not successful because they break rules.

One of the unfortunate side effects of this tension is that there can emerge a pattern of negativity aimed at top performers from their less successful colleagues. Beyond the fact that misery typically does love company, non-performers can tend to circle the wagons, a sort of collective rationalization for their underperformance. The negativity can take the form of water-cooler whispers, or more direct and outright condemnation, when the top performer is out of earshot or not present.

Robert Levin and Joseph Rosse wrote in *Talent Flow*:

Striving to maximize all employees' tenure is a dangerous ritual. Doing so ignores differences in performance among employees, and leads to keeping the good with the bad. In fact, at some point your better performers may seek another organization, one where performers count for more and they aren't stuck with coworkers who are non-performers or negative performers.

Allowing these sort of criticisms to continue is unfair to those being criticized, which is damaging to the culture of the organization and very bad for business. Nobody wants to be painted as a pariah, excluded from the club, or made the target of derision. While the top performers can seem to weather such criticisms better than most (a consequence of their resilience), the snide remarks, backhanded and thinly disguised humor, and outright meanness can take a toll. In the worst cases, top performers end up going someplace where they are made to feel more welcome.

A good manager will take charge when he or she notices this kind of behavior. They will stamp it out and ensure that all members of the team feel supported and encouraged and, more importantly, that there will be no tolerance for behavior and language that undermines colleagues.

Many years ago, I had a colleague complain to me about the habits of a sales rep that worked for us. "You know that Dennis spends half his time on the golf course," he said. To which I replied, "I couldn't care less where he spends his time as long as he continues to bring in the business." The rep in question was a longtime top salesman, and while I seriously doubt that he spent "half his time" on the golf course, he had certainly earned the right to have flexibility in his schedule.

One of my favorite sayings of his was that he made "radio calls." When I asked him what that meant, he said that it means you pull up to the retailer's store and a given song is playing on the car radio. You go inside, conduct your business, and return to the car, where you discover that the same song is still playing on the radio.

Again, while I doubt he conducted his business in the four or five minutes it took a song to play through on the radio, his point was that you don't get points for time spent with customers. You get in, conduct your business, and get out. Dennis may have been ahead of his time; Apple seems to work just like that today. You can go in, handle your business, and you're on your way in no time at all.

I stopped any criticism of Dennis in its tracks as nothing more than an attempt to undermine his valuable work so that someone else could feel better about their own lack of performance. To do otherwise would have condoned the insidious inference.

Challenge Your Salespeople

"The day you stop learning is the day you stop living."

—Richard Branson

Even the best salespeople need to be challenged. That should include measurable goal-setting and other tangibles, but it should also include challenging your people to continually expand their learning. There are so many resources available today, from books, blogs, TED Talks, YouTube, Twitter, LinkedIn, and a myriad of other opportunities that it is unconscionable to think that anyone would undertake improving themselves without committing to a habit of continuous learning.

As a manager, you should be serving up opportunities to learn on an ongoing basis. It could be something as simple as a TED Talk that you found interesting. It might be an article you read, or a blog you subscribe to. Creating a culture of learning has never been easier, and there has never been more available and relevant content. While it would be great to think that your salespeople are motivated to discover learning opportunities for themselves, the manager should, nonetheless, be a catalyst to provide content, and that can drive discussion and facilitate continued learning.

As we find ourselves deep in the midst of a massively changing retail landscape, the idea that anyone would manage today as he or she might have managed even five or ten years ago just makes no sense at all. Managers and salespeople must continue to work on their craft and seek learning opportunities from wherever they can get them. This can be done in small, digestible bites (Twitter, TED, books, etc.), and it can be done in larger doses, by taking continuing education courses at local universities and other learning institutions. No matter what, it has to be a part of what every salesperson does if they have aspire to excel in sales.

In 2002, a few weeks after I started working for the Boston-based diamond brand Hearts on Fire, Glenn Rothman, the founder and CEO, dropped a folder on my desk and asked me if I would like to do this. The "do this" part turned out to be the Key Executives Program at the Harvard Business School, and it was, needless to say, a magnificent experience. What Glenn had done in that one gesture was to announce that I had joined a learning organization. That his philosophy in that regard aligned so beautifully with my own was a very happy coincidence and one I cherished. At Christmas, instead of sending decorative tins of cookies or popcorn to our retail partners, we sent business books. Again, another statement about our culture of education.

Most small businesses don't have the resources to send their staff to the Harvard Business School. Every business, however, has the opportunity, indeed the obligation, to ensure that they are doing their part to further the education of their salespeople. This starts with the manager. He or she should create a curriculum of learning consisting of blogs, articles, YouTube videos, TED Talks, etc. There are also great learning experiences to be had by shopping other retail stores, both good and bad, in your particular category and otherwise. Give your team some parameters to assess, such as the way they are greeted, the kind of music playing in the store, anything unique about the lighting, particular scents that may have been present etc., etc.

Serve up some themes once or twice a week, and conduct meetings about the particular topics to discuss what everyone learned from them and how they might be used in the business. Nowadays, this can be done for practically no cost, save the time to find the content and the willingness to lead the conversation thereafter.

Brian Tracy wrote in *Be a Sales Superstar*, "We are experiencing an explosion of knowledge and technology that is unprecedented in human history. These advances are creating new competitors and driving our existing competition to better, faster, cheaper ways to get business. This is why continuous learning is the minimum requirement for success in selling today."

As the conversation between the CFO and the CEO goes, when the former asks the latter, "What happens if we train them and they leave?" to which the CEO responds, "What happens if we don't train them and they stay?"

Meritocracy

"Pay peanuts and you get monkeys."

—DAVID OGILVY

Jonah Berger wrote in *Contagious*:

> A few years ago, students at Harvard University were asked to make a seemingly straightforward choice: which would they prefer, a job where they made $50k a year (option A) or one where they made $100k a year (option B)? Seems like a no brainer, right? Everyone should take option B. But there was one catch. In option A, the students would get paid twice as much as others, who would only get $25K. In option B, they would get paid half as much as others, who would get $200k. So option B would make the students more money overall, but they would be doing worse than others around them. What did the majority of people choose? Option A. They preferred to do better than others, even if it meant getting less for themselves. They chose the option that was worse in absolute terms but better in relative terms. People don't just care about how they are doing; they care about their performance in relation to others.

As the Harvard study demonstrated, the relationship between key players and compensation is a very interesting one. Daniel Pink's central thesis in *Drive* is that compensation—commissions, bonuses, and other assorted carrots—is not always successful in driving the kinds of behaviors and performance that a company would like if the employees are not intrinsically motivated.

I know of many people who have given Pink's book a cursory read (or maybe they just heard about it!) and have decided to pay their teams a base salary, absent commissions and bonuses. Their takeaway seems to be that Pink is advocating against paying bonuses and commissions, and so they eliminate them in favor of straight salary.

Here's the problem with that proposition: what Pink is really saying is that no carrot will fix a problem that is really about intrinsic wiring. If the salesperson does not have the inherent wiring (drive) to perform at a high level, they are not going to acquire it by having a weekly, monthly, or annual incentive.

It's not a stretch to draw a comparison between Pink's *Drive* and my book *Hiring Squirrels* (other than one sold a billion copies and the other, well, didn't). They both speak to the inherent wiring of the salesperson; something, quite frankly, that is not changeable by exterior factors (commissions, bonuses, training, threats, etc.).

The second point that many advocates of Pink's work seem to forget is that he also said to take the issue of money off the table. In other words, pay your key performers enough money (however you choose to structure that) so that money ceases to be an issue. He was not, of course, suggesting that businesses bankrupt themselves to keep their performers happy, but that valued employees ought to be paid a little above the going rate so that you don't lose them.

Getting back to the Harvard study, what it shows is that top performers not only need to be paid well, they need to be paid fairly. They want to know that their compensation is commensurate with their performance *and* that it is appropriate as it relates to the pay of their less accomplished colleagues.

There are many businesses that have transparency in salaries. We can, of course, find out the compensation of top executives in public companies. We often hear about the exorbitant salaries paid to professional athletes, and it is not unusual to hear of large payments being made to actors and musicians. That level of transparency is not, however, typical in small businesses, and I'm not sure that it needs to be.

What I do believe, however, is that one thing must be patently clear to all of your salespeople, and that is that *the best performers will be paid more than those who are not performing as well*. Even as you protect the specifics of what that compensation is, it should be unapologetically clear that the best performing salespeople bring in more revenues than their colleagues—that's how you keep the lights on—and the pay structure will reflect that sense of priority.

I would be remiss not to offer one very important caveat to the top performers being paid the most, because they produce the goods that help to pay the electricity bill. They cannot give the product away. If they are discounting their way to sales, then they are not great salespeople, they ought not to be paid very well, and they are not doing your business any favors. Aside from that specific circumstance, pay your best salespeople well, and be unapologetically transparent with the rest of your team that your top performers will always make more money than those who do not perform as well.

And, lest you think I am both Irish *and* green, I know that there will always be a chorus of people arguing that while the top salespeople are busy selling, someone is cleaning up behind them and handling the stuff the top salespeople just don't want to do. I get it. I really do. So pay those people commensurate with those tasks, and remind them that they don't face the same challenges or deal with the same stresses that top salespeople bring to work (and home) every single day. I don't have to know how to fix a bus to be able to drive it, but someone better be doing the mechanical work, and someone needs to drive the bus.

And in the End . . .

I was giving a presentation to the management team of a multiple-door retail jewelry company recently, and when I asked if there were any questions, one of the managers said that she didn't buy it. She just didn't believe that salespeople didn't evolve and become better over a period of years. She was, of course, correct. People do evolve, they do learn, they do become better as a consequence of having lived and learned. That development can take the form of becoming more mature in how they handle people—customers, colleagues, bosses, and subordinates. They can become much wiser in how they handle internal conflict or customer complaints. They can develop into product and/or procedural experts as a result of being present and engaged in a given culture and company.

Sebastian Coe, the great British middle-distance runner, wrote in his biography, "Like many people I know, my education only really got going when I left full-time education." Our opportunities to learn and grow are, for some, as fundamental as food and shelter. For others, development can be an obligation or an obsession. To believe that human beings cannot develop and grow would be a very dark view of the human condition.

What we cannot do, however, is change our inherent wiring. If you believe otherwise, take a few moments to map out how you might change the personalities of your siblings or kids to reflect each other. If you have two kids, and one is an extrovert and one an introvert, good luck trying to switch that wiring. If you have a brother who has never been a good listener and a sister who has always been a great listener, the same good luck to you if you try to change your brother.

Randy Larsen and David Buss wrote in *Personality Psychology: Domains of Knowledge about Human Nature*:

> You might be wondering how the vast differences among people could be captured and represented by a few key personality traits. How is it that the uniqueness of every individual can be portrayed by just a few traits? Trait psychologists are somewhat like chemists.

They argue that, by combining a few primary traits in various amounts, they can distill the unique qualities of every individual. This process is analogous to that of combining the three primary colors. Every visible color in the spectrum, from dusty mauve to burnt umber, is created through various combinations of the three primary colors: red, green, and blue. According to trait psychologists, every personality, no matter how complex or unusual, is the product of a particular combination of a few basic and primary traits.

It doesn't really jive with our sense of what is possible to believe that people cannot change their inherent wiring, and yet that is precisely what we must come to grips with. If someone has low ego drive, it is likely to become more entrenched with the passage of time, not less. If they have low resilience, and seek to avoid situations where they may face rejection, that too is likely to become more of a factor as they age. And if you have someone who has demonstrated low empathy over the course of his life, he is not likely to become more empathic as a consequence of training, cajoling, or a new compensation package.

Herb Greenberg and Patrick Sweeney wrote in *How to Hire and Develop Your Next Top Performer:*

Appropriate development can make the inherently successful salesperson more productive. But people devoid of sales potential—for example, rigid, opinionated, and unempathic individuals—rarely respond to training, no matter how thorough and scientifically valid the training may be. People lacking ego-drive, those individuals who gain no personal gratification from the sales process or from closing a sale, are not likely to respond to sales development because they simply do not enjoy the process of persuading others. They may go through the motions prescribed by the instructors, but the long-term results are likely to be nil.

If those essential traits are present, and the Caliper organization suggests that about 25 percent of the general population has them, then there is a great deal of learning and development that can and must happen to make those people even more successful in sales. That wiring is a tremendous foundation to help you become successful if you do commit to what I described as *serial learning*, seeking every opportunity to build upon your natural wiring and your current skill set.

Understanding how to utilize the paradox of choice, the contrast principle, the idea of priming your customer, as we saw beautifully illustrated by Ricky Wubnig in the chapter on priming, should all be very useful insights.

Thinking about your own body language, how you might use your natural sense of humor, and how you might develop and appropriately utilize relevant stories to share with your customers should also be very helpful.

Watching how other top salespeople perform, and thinking about how you might benefit from creating your own language to tap into the customers' desire to not have any regrets about their choices, can be great tools in your professional development.

If you have the wiring and the desire to be an outstanding performer in sales, nothing can stop you but the limits you impose upon yourself. For me, watching outstanding salespeople at work is, and always has been, a great privilege. They operate on a different plane than the rest of us, and they are no different than the very best practitioners in any field or profession you can think of.

If this book contributed in some small measure to helping you understand sales principles and approaches, if it gave you a few ideas to add to your own skill set, or if it helped you understand some of the challenges in recognizing and managing salespeople, then I will consider my journey in writing this book to have been worthwhile. Thanks for your time, and feel free to drop me a line anytime.

Peter Smith
Canton, Massachusetts —
November 2016

Contact Information:

If you enjoyed this book and you would like to read additional articles, get related links, and enjoy other material I write and share, feel free to connect with me on any of the following:

Facebook: *Hiring Squirrels*
LinkedIn: Peter Smith
Twitter: Peter Smith @HiringSquirrels
Dublinsmith@Yahoo.com
www.hiringsquirrels.com

Hiring Squirrels and *Sell Something* are both available on Amazon.com in paperback and Kindle editions.

For inquiries related to speaking engagements, please use the email above.

Works Cited

Anand, Sahir. "Changing the Retail Labor Model for a New Retail Environment—EKN Research." *EKN Research*. N.p., 10 Feb. 2016. http://eknresearch.com/2016/02/05/changing-the-retail-labor-model-for-a-new-retail-environment/ Accessed 10 Sept. 2016. Web.

Anders, George. *The Rare Find: Spotting Exceptional Talent before Everyone Else*. New York: Portfolio/Penguin, 2011. Print.

Bannister, Roger. *The Four-Minute Mile*. New York: Dodd, Mead, 1955. Print.

Berger, Jonah. *Contagious: Why Things Catch On*. New York: Simon & Schuster, 2013. Print.

Botton, Alain de. *Status Anxiety*. New York: Pantheon, 2004. Print.

Brewer, Geoffrey, and Barb Sanford. *The Best of the Gallup Management Journal, 2001–2007*. New York: Gallup, 2007. Print.

Broughton, Philip Delves. *The Art of the Sale: Learning from the Masters about the Business of Life*. New York: Penguin, 2012. Print.

Buckingham, Marcus, and Curt Coffman. *First, Break All the Rules: What the World's Greatest Managers Do Differently*. New York.: Simon & Schuster, 1999. Print.

Buckingham, Marcus, and Donald O. Clifton. *Now, Discover Your Strengths*. New York: Free Press, 2001. Print.

Cain, Susan. *Quiet: The Power of Introverts in a World That Can't Stop Talking*. New York: Crown Publishers, 2012. Print.

Carlson, Kurt A. and Suzanne B. Shu. "When Three Charms but Four Alarms: Identifying the Optimal Number of Claims in Persuasion Settings." *Journal of Marketing* 78.1 (June 10, 2013). Available at SSRN: http://ssrn.com/abstract=2277117 or http://dx.doi.org/10.2139/ssrn.2277117

Cespedes, Frank V. *Aligning Strategy and Sales: The Choices, Systems, and Behaviors That Drive Effective Selling.* Boston: Harvard Business Review Press, 2014. Print.

Cialdini, Robert B. *Influence: The Psychology of Persuasion.* New York: Collins, 2007. Print.

Collins, James C. *Good to Great: Why Some Companies Make the Leap . . . and Others Don't.* New York, NY: Harper Business, 2001. Print.

Colvin, Geoffrey. *Talent Is Overrated: What Really Separates World-Class Performers from Everybody Else.* New York: Portfolio, 2008. Print.

Demarais, Ann, and Valerie White. *First Impressions: What You Don't Know About How Others See You.* New York: Bantam, 2004.

Derlega, Valerian J., Barbara A. Winstead, and Warren H. Jones. *Personality: Contemporary Theory and Research.* Chicago: Nelson-Hall, 1991. Print.

Dieken, Connie. *Talk Less, Say More: 3 Habits to Influence Others and Make Things Happen.* Hoboken, NJ: Wiley, 2010. Print.

Dixon, Matthew, Nick Toman, and Rick DeLisi. *The Effortless Experience: Conquering the New Battleground for Customer Loyalty.* New York: Portfolio/Penguin New York, 2013. Print.

"Fewer Mothers Prefer Full-time Work." *Pew Research Centers Social Demographic Trends Project RSS*. N.p., 12 July 2007. http://www.pewsocialtrends.org/2007/07/12/fewer-mothers-prefer-full-time-work/ Accessed 11 Sept. 2016. Web.

Gilbert, Daniel Todd. *Stumbling on Happiness*. New York: A.A. Knopf, 2006. Print.

Goleman, Daniel. *Emotional Intelligence:* New York: Bantam, 2006. Print.

Grant, A. M. "Rethinking the Extraverted Sales Ideal: The Ambivert Advantage." *Psychological Science* 24.6 (2013): 1024–30. Web.

Grant, Adam M. *Give and Take: A Revolutionary Approach to Success*. New York: Viking, 2013. Print.

Greenberg, Herb, Patrick Sweeney, and Harold Weinstein. *How to Hire and Develop Your Next Top Performer: The Five Qualities That Make Salespeople Great*. New York: McGraw-Hill, 2001. Print.

Guber, Peter. *Tell to Win: Connect, Persuade, and Triumph with the Hidden Power of Story*. New York: Crown Business, 2011. Print.

Hall, Freeman. *Retail Hell: How I Sold My Soul to the Store: Confessions of a Tortured Sales Associate*. Avon, MA: Adams Media, 2009. Print.

"Hay Group Study Finds Employee Turnover in Retail Industry Is Slowly Increasing." *Hay Group RSS*. N.p., n.d. Web. 11 Sept. 2016.

Iyengar, Sheena. *The Art of Choosing*. New York: Twelve, 2010. Print.

Jamail, Nathan. *The Sales Professionals Playbook*. Frisco, TX: Scooter, 2011. Print.

Kahneman, Daniel. *Thinking, Fast and Slow*. New York: Farrar, Straus and Giroux, 2011. Print.

Kay, Eddy. *Thriving in the Shadow of Giants: How to Find Success as an Independent Retailer*. West Hollywood, CA: Armarium, 2002. Print.

Knight, Philip H. *Shoe Dog: A Memoir by the Creator of Nike*. New York: Scribner/S&S, 2016. Print.

Lal, Rajiv, Jose B. Alvarez, and Dan Greenberg. *Retail Revolution: Will Your Brick & Mortar Store Survive?* Self-published, 2014.

Levin, Robert, and Joseph G. Rosse. *Talent Flow: A Strategic Approach to Keeping Good Employees, Helping Them Grow, and Letting Them Go*. San Francisco: Jossey-Bass, 2001. Print.

Lewis, David. *Impulse: Why We Do What We Do without Knowing Why We Do It*. Cambridge, MA: Belknap Press, 2013. Print.

Lewis, Marc D. *The Biology of Desire: Why Addiction Is Not a Disease*. Canada: Doubleday, 2015. Print.

Lewis, Robin, and Michael Dart. *The New Rules of Retail: Competing in the World's Toughest Marketplace*. New York: Palgrave Macmillan, 2010. Print.

Lindstrom, Martin. *Buyology: Truth and Lies about Why We Buy*. New York: Doubleday, 2008. Print.

Lindstrom, Martin. *Small Data: The Tiny Clues That Uncover Huge Trends*. New York: St. Martin's Press, 2016. Print.

Lyubomirsky, Sonja. *The Myths of Happiness: What Should Make You Happy but Doesn't, What Shouldn't Make You Happy but Does.* New York: Penguin, 2014. Print.

Martin, Rod A. *The Psychology of Humor: An Integrative Approach.* Amsterdam: Elsevier Academic, 2007. Print.

Miller, Alan S., and Satoshi Kanazawa. *Why Beautiful People Have More Daughters: From Dating, Shopping, and Praying to Going to War and Becoming a Billionaire: Two Evolutionary Psychologists Explain Why We Do What We Do.* New York: Perigee, 2007. Print.

Mlodinow, Leonard. *Subliminal: How Your Unconscious Mind Rules Your Behavior.* New York: Pantheon, 2012. Print.

Montville, Leigh. *The Big Bam: The Life and Times of Babe Ruth.* New York: Doubleday, 2006. Print.

Mukherjee, Siddhartha. *The Gene: An Intimate History.* New York: Scribner, 2016. Print.

O'Connell, Sanjida. *Mindreading: An Investigation into How We Learn to Love and Lie.* New York: Doubleday, 1998. Print.

Ogilvy, David. *Confessions of an Advertising Man.* New York: Atheneum, 1963. Print.

Pink, Daniel H. *Drive: The Surprising Truth about What Motivates Us.* New York: Riverhead, 2009. Print.

Pink, Daniel H. *To Sell Is Human: The Surprising Truth about Moving Others.* New York: Riverhead, 2012. Print.

Porath, Christopher, and Christine Pearson. "The Price of Incivility." *Harvard Business Review*. (January-February 2013) https://hbr.org/2013/01/the-price-of-incivility Accessed: 10 Sept. 2016. Web.

Postema, Dennis. *Psychology of Sales: From Average to Rainmaker: Using the Power of Psychology to Increase Sales.* CreateSpace, 2013. Print.

Poundstone, William. *Priceless: The Myth of Fair Value (and How to Take Advantage of It).* New York: Hill and Wang, 2010. Print.

Raynor, Michael E., and Mumtaz Ahmed. *The Three Rules: How Exceptional Companies Think.* New York: Portfolio/Penguin, 2013. Print.

Robertson, Ian H. *The Winner Effect: How Power Affects Your Brain.* London: Bloomsbury, 2012. Print.

Rond, Mark de. *There Is an I in Team: What Elite Athletes and Coaches Really Know about High Performance.* Boston, MA: Harvard Business Review, 2012. Print.

Rosen, Bob. *Grounded: How Leaders Stay Rooted in an Uncertain World.* San Francisco: Jossey-Bass, 2014. Print.

Rosen, Keith. *Coaching Salespeople into Sales Champions: A Tactical Playbook for Managers and Executives.* Hoboken, NJ: John Wiley & Sons, 2008. Print.

Schwartz, Barry. *The Paradox of Choice: Why More Is Less.* New York: Ecco, 2004. Print.

Sharma, Robin S. *The Leader Who Had No Title: A Modern Fable on Real Success in Business and in Life.* New York: Free Press, 2010. Print.

Stephens, Doug. *The Retail Revival: Reimagining Business for the New Age of Consumerism*. Ontario: John Wiley, 2013. Print.

Suggs, Steve. *Can They Sell: Learn to Recruit the Best Salespeople*. N.p.: InLight, 2014. Print.

Tracy, Brian. *Be a Sales Superstar: 21 Great Ways to Sell More, Faster, Easier, in Tough Markets*. San Francisco: Berrett-Koehler, 2002. Print.

Willis, J., and A. Todorov. "First Impressions: Making Up Your Mind After a 100-Ms Exposure to a Face." *Psychological Science* 17.7 (2006): 592–98. Web.

Ziglar, Zig. *Zig Ziglar's Secrets of Closing the Sale*. Old Tappan, NJ: F.H. Revell, 1984. Print.